Main Areas
1. Eston Nab
2. Highcliffe N
3. Easby Moor
4. Kildale
5. Ingleby Greenhow
6. Hasty Bank Area
7. Scugdale
8. Ingleby Arncliffe
9. Peak Scar
10. Whitestonecliffe
11. Eskdale Area

f. Tripsdale
g. Oak Crag
h. Middle Head
i. Esklets
j. Thorgill
k. Bridestones

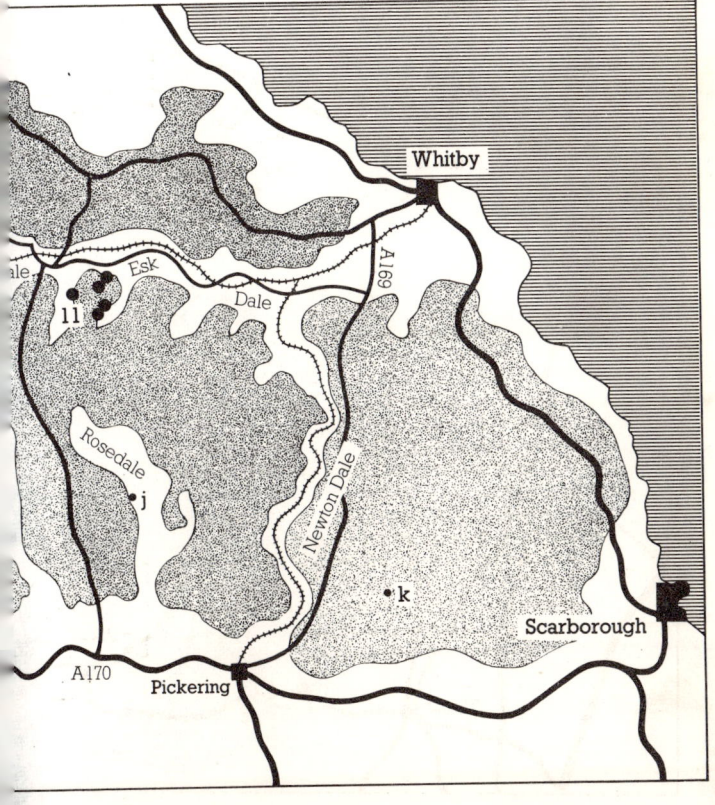

Rock Climbs on the

NORTH YORK MOORS

Cleveland Mountaineering Club

Les Barker
Steve Brown
Nick Dixon
Ian Dunn
Rick Graham
Paul Ingham
Ken Jackson
Dave McKinney
Kelvin Neal
Stuart Patterson
Dave Paul
John Redhead
Chris Shorter
Pete Simcock
Mike Statham
Chris Woodall

Maps by Ivan Cumberpatch

Published by **CORDEE** Leicester

Climbs in Cleveland 1956 by M.F. Wilson
Climbs on the North York Moors 1961 M.F. Wilson
North York Moors Climbers' Guide 1970 A Marr

© The Cleveland Mountaineering Club/Cordee 1985

Simcock, Peter
　Rock climbs on the North York Moors.—4th ed.
　1. Rock climbing—England—North York Moors
　(North Yorkshire)
　I. Title
　796.5'223'0942846　　GV199.44.G72N6
　ISBN 0-904405-92-3

Produced by the Ernest Press, Glasgow G44 5QD.

Front cover: Stratagem, Raven's Scar, Paul Ingham
　　　　　　Photo: Stu Bradley

Back cover: Nightwatch, Whitestonecliffe, Stu Bradley
　　　　　　Photo: John Philpott

This guide book is available from all specialist climbing shops
and book shops within the area, or direct from the publishers
CORDEE 3a DeMontfort Street, Leicester, LE1 7HD

CONTENTS
Page No.

AREA MAP	Inside Covers
INTRODUCTION and ACKNOWLEDGEMENTS	5
TECHNICAL INFORMATION	6
RECOMMENDED ROUTES	7
USE OF AID	8
GENERAL INFORMATION	8
ACCESS INFORMATION	9
RESCUE AND SAFETY	10

MAIN AREAS

Eston Nab	11
Highcliffe Nab	17
Easby Moor Area	25
Kildale	33
Ingleby Greenhow Area	38
Hasty Bank Area	52
Scugdale Area	72
Ingleby Arncliffe	93
Peak Scar	98
Whitestonecliffe	113
Eskdale Area	127

OTHER CRAGS

Roseberry Topping	138
Cringle Crag	139
Silton	142
Kepwick	143
Tranmire Rocks	144
Tripsdale	148
Oak Crag	149
Middle Head	151
Esklets	152
Thorgill	154
Bridestones	156
Newtondale	159

DIAGRAMS

	Page No.
Cook's Crags	28
Park Nab	32
Raven's Scar	55
The Wainstones (Broughton Face)	64
The Wainstones (Bilsdale Face)	68
Scot Crags (Nos. 1-38)	74
Drunken Buttress	78
Pisa Buttress	78
Scugdale Buttress	78
Barker's Buttress	80
Holly Tree Buttress	80
Scot Crags (Nos. 67-76)	81
Barker's Crags	83
Stoney Wicks	88
Peak Scar (East Wall)	100
Peak Scar (Main Wall)	104
Whitestonecliffe (Nos. 1-11)	112
Whitestonecliffe (Nos. 11-20)	116
Whitestonecliffe (Nos. 24-38)	120

MAPS

Eston Nab	11
Highcliff	16
Easby Moor	16
Park Nab	16
Ingleby Greenhow Area	37
Hasty Bank	52
Scugdale	72
Ingleby Arncliffe	92
Peak Scar	98
Whitestone	113
Danby Area	126

Introduction

Rock climbing has taken place on the outcrops of North Yorkshire since 1906 and there has been much development since then. New crags have been discovered, whilst the original rocks are still being enjoyed by local climbers, their lines and challenges being met and overcome by successive generations.

The rocks have been documented and their routes described in three previous guides. The first, written and edited by Maurice Wilson, was published in 1956 and entitled "Climbs in Cleveland". This was followed in 1961 by "Climbs on the North York Moors", again produced by Maurice Wilson. The third, with the abbreviated title of "North York Moors" was written and edited by Tony Marr and published by West Col in 1970.

Since then standards have risen and this guide incorporates the new grading system to cover the more difficult climbs in the area. It is interesting to note that the grades of many of the original artificial routes have been changed from A to E and that many of the crags are now completely "free".

It is hoped that climbers will continue to enjoy and develop the North York Moors and that future routes will provide as much pleasure and satisfaction as those experienced by previous generations.

ACKNOWLEDGEMENTS

The present guide has combined the work of many people. We are in debt to Maurice Wilson and Tony Marr for their previous guides of which this one is, of course, merely an extension.

The work for this guide began in 1978 when Stuart Patterson formed a guidebook committee. Ian Dunn then took over its responsibility and completed the majority of the work. Chris Shorter, Rick Graham, Dave McKinney, Nick Dixon and Paul Ingham helped with the completion of the sandstone section and Steve Brown then finalised the limestone crags. He and Ian Dunn, helped by Kelvin Neal, Dave Paul and many others then added the most recent developments.

The following is a list of those who also have contributed to making this guide possible and we must apologise to anyone whose name has been inadvertently omitted.

Les Barker   Pete Simcock
Ken Jackson   Mike Statham
John Redhead   Chris Woodall

and the 1983 Cleveland Mountaineering Club committee.

We are also indebted to
Marjorie Chadwick   Karen Lake
Wendy Crawford-Smith   Julie Manton
Judith Cresswell   Diana Tweddle
Rosemary Hay

for typing and re-typing the drafts.

TECHNICAL INFORMATION
Adjectival Grade

This is a subjective assessment of the overall difficulty and seriousness of a route. It takes into consideration the quality of the rock, the exposure, the protection, the technical difficulty, its seriousness and the sustained nature of the route. It is assumed that climbers carry a comprehensive selection of protection devices and that the route is in good condition. The grades used are: abbreviated in the text:

Moderate	Mod.
Difficult	Diff.
Very Difficult	V. Diff.
Mild Severe	Mild Severe
Severe	Severe
Hard Severe	Hard Severe
Mild Very Severe	Mild V.S.
Very Severe	V.S.
Hard Very Severe	Hard V.S.

E1, E2, E3, E4, E5 (E meaning Extremely Severe)

Technical Grade

The technical grade is an objective assessment of the cumulative difficulty of a pitch, and as such considers the strenuousness and sustained nature of the climbing up to and after the crux. There is no definite relationship between the technical grade and the adjectival grade.

The grades used are:
4a 4b 4c
5a 5b 5c
6a 6b etc. the system being open ended.

Approximate equivalents can be:

Hard Severe	4b
Very Severe	4c or 5a
Hard Very Severe	4c, 5a or 5b
E1	5a, 5b or 5c
E2	5b or 5c
E3	5b, 5c, 6a or 6b
E4	5c, 6a or 6b
E5	6a or 6b

The climbs are graded for "on sight" leads but some of the harder routes have not been led without some prior knowledge. If in doubt seek local opinion.

Artificial Grades

Climbing involving artificial aid is classified in the traditional way. The grades used are:
    A1
    A2
    A3 etc.

RECOMMENDED ROUTES

A star grading system has been used; 3 stars denoting the best routes. For visitors to the area a list of recommended routes in the various grades is given.

Grade	Route	Crag	Page No.
Moderate	Needle	The Wainstones	63
Difficult	Tumble Down Dick	Raven's Scar	59
Very Difficult	North West Route	Highcliffe	18
	The Slab Climb	The Wainstones	70
	Jordu	Peak Scar	102
Severe	Sphinx Nose Traverse	The Wainstones	69
	Highcliffe Crack	Highcliffe	20
	Twin Cracks	Park Nab	34
Hard Severe	Forest Face	Raven's Scar	58
	Gone	Peak Scar	106
	Night Watch	Whitestonecliffe	123
Very Severe	Flake Crack	Highcliffe	19
	Telstar	Raven's Scar	61
	Frenesi	Peak Scar	107
Hard Very Severe	Wombat	Highcliffe	21
	Gehenna	Beacon Scar	97
	Styx	Park Nab	34
	Concave Wall	The Wainstones	70
	Fifi	Peak Scar	102
	Central Cracks	Whitestonecliffe	122
E1	Satchmo	Raven's Scar	56
	Ali Baba	The Wainstones	71
	Black Mamba	Whitestonecliffe	117
E2	Mongol	Beacon Scar	94
	Tremor	" "	97
	Fever Pitch	Raven's Scar	59
E3	Shere Khan	Park Nab	34
	Stargazer	Highcliffe	20
	Lemming Slab	The Wainstones	71
E4	Terrorist	The Wainstones	69
	Moonflower	Highcliffe	20
	Stratagem	Raven's Scar	57
E5	Magic in the Air	Highcliffe	20

USE OF AID

On some climbs pitons for protection have previously been used but most of these have now been removed. In such cases the position of the original peg is stated in the text.

It is generally accepted that the pegging of free routes is to be deplored as this damages the rock and spoils the climbs for others. So far bolts have never been used to protect free routes on the North York Moors and it is hoped that this high ethical standard may be maintained.

Chalk is in regular use on the routes and indeed many of the harder routes have not been climbed without its aid. However, it is hoped that climbers will use chalk sparingly to prevent unnecessary annoyance to "non-users".

Of course the chipping of holds on sandstone crags is the most deplorable practice of all and the North York Moors can well do without this atrocious form of vandalism.

GENERAL INFORMATION

The pitches in this guide have been described in the simplest terms, the directions left and right meaning when facing the crag. Unless otherwise stated the routes are described from left to right.

All grid references refer to the Ordnance Survey maps of the North York Moors. An explanation of the usage of a grid reference number appears at the foot of the map.

ACCESS INFORMATION

Most of the crags in this guide lie within the North York Moors National Park, an area designated for its natural beauty. It is controlled in order to conserve that beauty for the enjoyment and recreation of visitors to the area. Despite the term "national park", the majority of land in the park is privately owned. There are limited rights of public access, particularly the network of public rights of way. However, there exists no right of access to climb on the majority of crags. The fact that this guide includes a description of a crag or climb does not indicate a right to climb. We are therefore very dependent upon the tolerance and goodwill of landowners. It is essential that in order to preserve the valued freedoms of access, climbers respect the rights and wishes of the inhabitants and other visitors. It is the responsibility of climbers to take care not to pollute, destroy or damage the environment others also wish to enjoy. Below are some guidelines that should be adhered to:

1. Follow the description for access at the beginning of each section. If in doubt over footpaths, follow the public rights of way.

2. Do not climb walls or fences.

3. Do not leave litter and please remove any you may find.

4. Keep dogs on a leash.

5. Do not start fires.

6. When parking, try to avoid causing an obstruction, avoid gates, narrow lanes, drives etc.

7. If requested to leave by a land-owner then it may be wise in the long term interest of free access to leave with the minimum of fuss. If such access difficulties are encountered, it is helpful for later negotiations to obtain as much information as possible about ownership and the reasons for refusal of access.

The British Mountaineering Council, through its North East Area Committee, represents climbers' interests in maintaining access. It would help this committee considerably to be informed of any access problems, or of situations such as litter or damaged fences, that might give rise to access difficulties. Information can be forwarded via the local climbing clubs or the

>British Mountaineering Council,
>Crawford House,
>Precinct Centre,
>Booth St. East,
>Manchester M13 9RZ.
>
>Tel: 061 273 5835

10 INTRODUCTION

A great deal of work, patience and negotiation can be ruined by bad manners, selfishness and disrespect shown by a few climbers. Providing we endeavour to apply the above code, it is likely we may continue to climb in this beautiful area.

RESCUE AND SAFETY

Two rescue teams operate on the North York Moors, one based in the Teesside area and the other at Scarborough. Both can be called out by the police but may also be contacted direct by phoning:

> Stokesley 712462 or
> Scarborough 870320

The following notes are only intended as a simple guide to first aid procedure until help arrives.

Stop any bleeding by applying a firm dressing or by direct pressure to the wound.

Do not move the injured person if you suspect a spinal injury.

Support and rest any broken limb, but do not straighten it.

Keep the injured person warm and comfortable.

If the injured person is unconscious, check breathing and pulse. If not present start mouth to mouth resuscitation and external cardiac massage. Otherwise lay the person on his side and check his mouth is clear of obstruction.

Exposure has an insiduous onset and is often not recognised at an early stage. Slurred speech, stumbling and irrational behaviour should alert one to the possibility. Find shelter, apply warm dry clothing and give hot drinks if available.

Adder bites are treated by immobilising the affected part and keeping the injured person still.

ESTON NAB 11

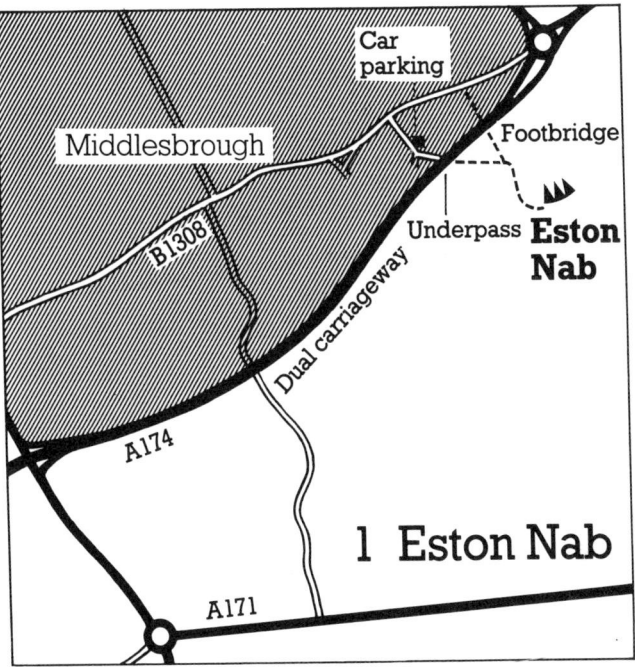

Eston Nab
G.R. 566183

Eston Nab lies immediately above the A174 (Parkway) above the town of Eston. It can easily be defined by a monument above the rocks. The crags are in a prominent position overlooking Teesside and the Tees estuary and are best approached by following the A174 to the roundabout just east of Eston. Follow the road back west towards Eston and take the first turning on the left (into a housing estate). Follow the road south until a small parking space can be found near to a footbridge over the A174. Cross this and ascend direct to the rocks passing some mine buildings.

Eston Nab is probably the most unattractively situated crag in the North York Moors and greatest care should be exercised with equipment left at the bottom of routes.

HISTORY

Eston Nab has been climbed on for many years, certainly since the 1930's, but it was not until J. Hickman and T. Sullivan recorded a number of routes in the 1950's that its potential was realised. Soon after the 1961 guide G. Fixter and E. Marr climbed many of the remaining blanks. (Some routes appear to have chipped holds and this practice is to be deplored).

BARE FACE

This is a steep wall approximately 75 yds right of where the footpath reaches the crag. The face can be defined by a line of bolt holes in the middle of the wall and a prominent zig-zag crack on the right.

Left of Bare Face are numerous rocks with problems on them. These were recorded in a previous edition of this guide but due to rock falls and the shortness of the routes they have been found unworthy of inclusion. Nearly all obvious lines fall below severe.

Chaser Chimney   15ft.   Diff.
The obvious corner crack to the left of the Bare Face.

Bare Face Robbery   15ft.   Hard Severe (4b)
Start right of Chaser Chimney. Climb the wall direct. A good route.

Small Holding   20ft.   Hard VS (5b)
Climb wall right of Bare Face Robbery on chipped bolt holes.

Zig-Zag   25ft.   Severe
The crack right of Small Holding.

When Carlos Strums His Banjo   20ft.   Hard VS (5b)
From the start of Zig-Zag step right. Climb the arete and slab to the top.

Introductory Slab   25ft.   Mod.
The slabs ten feet right of Zig-Zag.

Pirate Ridge   20ft.   Diff.
Start right of skull and crossbones carved in the rock. Climb ridge and overhanging block at the top.

Orange Peel   20ft.   Hard V.S. (5a)
Climb the wall 5ft. right of Pirate Ridge.

Communism   15ft.   V.S. (5a)
Start 5ft. right of Orange Peel in a corner left of a small overhang. The corner is climbed with difficulty.

NORTH FACE

Oliver's Overhang　15ft.　Mild V.S. (4c)
The corner to the right of Communism and the wall above.

Bilberry Crack　15ft.　Diff.
The short crack 12ft. right of Oliver's Overhang.

Staircase　20ft.　Mod.
5ft. right of Bilberry Crack go diagonally left up the wall.

Stair Carpet　20ft.　Diff.
Start as for Staircase but go diagonally right up the wall.

Simplex　25ft.　Hard V. Diff.
Start 10ft. right of Staircase. The wall is climbed on small holds.

GREAT WALL

Peleton　25ft.　V.S. (4c)
The obvious corner crack is climbed throughout. A good route.

Too Simplex　25ft.　V.S. (4c)
Start 5ft. right of Peleton. Climb the wall direct passing a ledge.

The Bobet Traverse　70ft.　V.S. (4b)
Start 30ft. right of Peleton at the junction of the North and West faces of the Great Wall. Climb the edge obliquely to the start of Peleton. Traverse the obvious horizontal ledge to the right, turn the corner, move right until it is possible to drop down onto a large flake. Follow this into the corner capped by an overhang and finish by climbing the right hand side of the overhang.

Brown Sugar　45ft.　V.S. (4c)
Climb the obvious corner crack approximately 20ft. right of the corner. Ascend the crack and the wall above, (which lives up to its name).

Grandstand　50ft.　Hard V.S. (5b)
Start as for Brown Sugar. Climb this route until a line of pockets can be followed left to the arete. Finish up this.

Great Chimney　45ft.　Hard V. Diff.
The obvious flake and chimney route in the centre of the West face. Start up the flake to a large ledge, and climb the awkward chimney above.

Mercier　45ft.　Hard V.S. (5a)　*
Start right of the Great Chimney. Ascend the wall to the top of the flake. Move right and ascend direct.

Maillot Jaune   45ft.   V.S. (4c)   *
Start in the corner right of Mercier. Climb up to the final overhang. Move out left to finish.

MA   45ft.   V. Diff.
The obvious gulley 25ft. right of Maillot Jaune finishing up its right fork. The left fork is severe and very sandy.

Crack and Flake   40ft.   Diff.
10ft. right of MA.

Across the grass slope is:-

TRIPARTITE WALL

Mafac   30ft.   E1 (5b)
The left hand of the two obvious chimneys.

Mafac Right Hand   35ft.   Hard V.S. (5a)
The crack just right of Mafac is climbed. Finish to the left or direct.

The Grippa   35ft.   Hard V.S. (5a)
10ft. right of Mafac below an overhanging scoop, climb the scoop to a ledge, step left and follow the crack to the top.

Via Marie   25ft.   Severe
Start up corner to right of right-hand chimney, up the corner, till a traverse left can be made up again to finish.

Lliwedd Crack   25ft.   Severe
Start as for Via Maria. Climb the outside of the chimney.

Concrete Crack   25ft.   Severe
Climb the crack 10ft. right of Lliwedd Crack.

Scoop Crack   25ft.   Mild V.S. (4b)
Climb the overhanging corner 5ft. right of Concrete Crack.

ZERO WALL

Udda   30ft.   Hard V.S. (5a)
Start as for Zero Traverse and climb direct to the top.

Combined Ops.   30ft.   Hard Severe (4b)
The crack in the centre of Zero Wall.

Zero Traverse   30ft.   Hard Severe (4b)
Start as for scoop crack and traverse to Combined Ops. Finish as for that route.

WATCHTOWER BUTTRESS

Bennison's Chimney   30ft.   Hard V. Diff.
Climb the diagonal crack and chimney above.

Bennison's Crack   30ft.   Hard V. Diff.
Climb the thin crack 10ft. right of Bennison's Chimney. Finish as for that route.

PA   30ft.   Hard V. Diff.
Climb the short arete 20ft. right of the previous route.

Pafrendo   30ft.   Severe
Start as above. Move right and ascend twin crack to the top.

Pafrendo Direct   20ft.   V.S. (4c)
Start at the thin crack 8ft. right of the ordinary start. Climb the crack direct and finish as for the ordinary route.

WILTON CORNER

Crystal Wall   25ft.   Severe
Immediately to the left of the undercut wall. Climb obliquely to the left on crystal holds.

Wilton Wall   25ft.   Hard Severe (4b)
As for Crystal Wall but straight up on good holds after an awkward start.

Trog   25ft.   Hard Severe (4b)
The right arete of Wilton Wall.

Sixty feet right of Wilton Corner is an isolated buttress with two routes.

Secret Groove   15ft.   Hard V.S. (5b)
Ascend the obvious groove with difficulty.

Unknown Buttress   15ft.   Hard Severe (4b)
Start 5ft. right of Secret Groove. Ascend the curving crack on delicate holds.

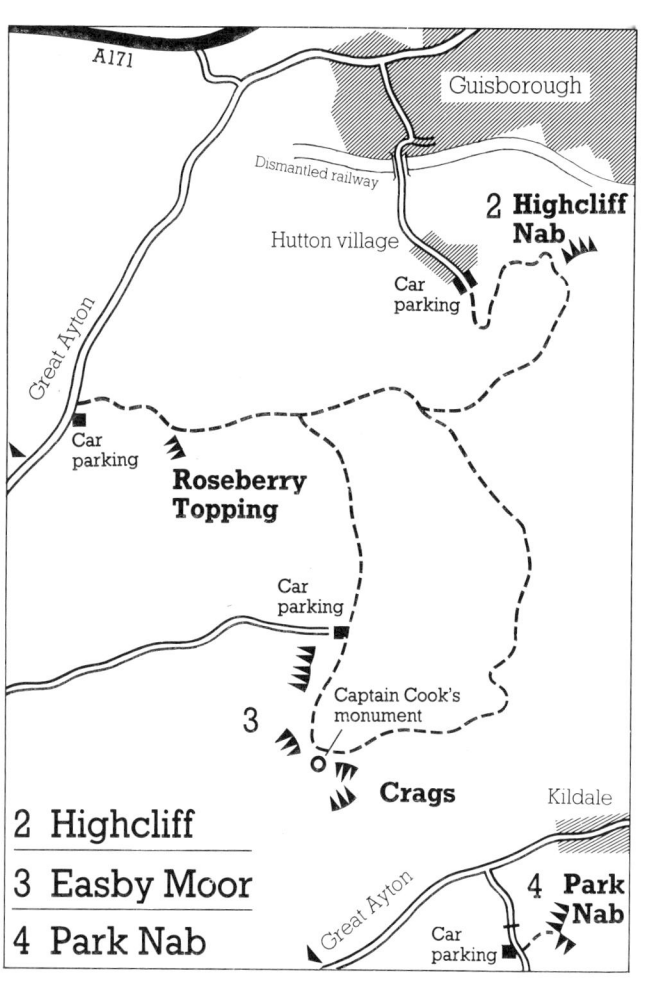

Highcliffe Nab GR 610138

This expanse of rock, very prominent on the Moors to the south of Guisborough, is best reached from Hutton Low Cross where a track leaving the south end of the village takes one to the rocks in little more than twenty minutes. Alternatively the Nab may be reached from the southern perimeters of Guisborough by following the paths which lead from the housing estates.

The rocks are steep and the climbs tend to follow natural lines in some fine positions. The exposure is great at all times. Unfortunately there is a paucity of belays and the finish of some of the climbs, especially on the west face, require care.

The crag is quite extensive varying from 15ft. to 60ft. in height. The rock itself is sandstone, tending to give pleasant climbing in the summer months. However in winter months the crag is often lichen covered and wet.

HISTORY

Highcliffe Nab was discovered in the early 1930's and most of the standard V. Diffs. and Severes were climbed by the Barker Brothers and their colleagues. Some thirty years later, D. Holliday made an outstanding contribution with the fine Scarecrow crack, and in 1966 Les Brown eliminated the aid on Wombat, thus producing the best Hard V.S. on the crag. During the early seventies many new routes were added, including Flange Crack by Hugh Banner and D. Larkins, to be followed in 1977 by the impressive wall climbs, Trampled Underfoot and Rockhopper by R. Graham and D. McKinney. More recently, a number of significantly harder routes have appeared; notably Cardiac Arrest by Kelvin Neal, Moonflower by Dave Paul, and the hard and bold Magic in the Air by Nick Dixon.

WEST FACE

All climbs are described from right to left.

Ladies First   50ft.   Hard V. Diff.
Start at a crack 10ft. left of a cross carved on the rock. Climb the crack, traverse right for 10ft. round a protrusion to the foot of a curving crack, which is climbed to a platform. Continue diagonally right up a series of small ledges to the final crumbling rocks which lead to the top.

Direct Start   20ft.   V.S. (4c)
Start at the cross carved in the rock. Ascend the short awkward wall to the junction with the ordinary route. Another variation can be made a few feet further right.

Gardom 45ft. V.S. (4c)
Start up the initial crack of Ladies First then climb the crack in the final headwall.

Somorrah 45ft. V.S. (4c)
Climb the arete left of Gardom.

Isolation 50ft. V.Diff.
Start up the initial crack of Ladies First to a broad ledge. Cross the ledge to a niche known as 'Isolation Corner'. Traverse left to a small buttress which is climbed to the 'Gallery'. Traverse right round a bulge and gain the moor above.

West Face Route 80ft. Diff.
Start 40ft. right of the NW corner of the crag. Climb a short right angled corner followed by slabby rocks to a wide ledge. Traverse right to a 10ft. wall. Climb the wall to the 'Balcony'. Make an awkward move to the 'Gallery' above. Finish from the left end of the 'Gallery'. Numerous variations up to severe can be made.

No Hiding Place 35ft. E2 (5c)
Start just to the left of West Face Route. Gain a small mantle-shelf then follow a line of thin cracks and shattered rock directly up the wall passing a small niche. The rock is poor.

Variation 40ft. Hard Severe(4b)
Start as for ordinary route. Climb the first thin crack for 10ft. Step left and gain a small ledge. Finish as for NW route.

Jeff's Variation 20ft. Hard V.S. (4c)
Start 10ft. left of West Face route, climb the bulging wall to a junction with NW route.

North West Direct 30ft. V.S. (4c) *
Start 10ft. right of North West Route. Climb the faint crack line direct to an exposed corner. Climb the slab and crack in the nose of the corner to the top. A good pitch.

North West Route 45ft. V. Diff. *
Start 15ft. right of the north west corner of the crag. Climb a square groove and slab leading to an exposed corner, gain a small ledge then traverse round the arete to the right to a flake crack, climb direct to the top. A fine route.

HIGHCLIFFE NAB

NORTH FACE

Highcliff Chimney (Ordinary)   50ft.   V. Diff.
Start from the north west corner of the nab. An obvious 'scoop' on the corner followed by easy ledges lead to a shelf on the right wall of the chimney. Stride on to the left wall and gain access to the chimney. Climb strenuously past the jammed boulders. An exit is made over the right wall.

Highcliff Chimney (Direct)   40ft.   Severe
Enter the chimney at its base and back and foot up to join the ordinary route at the 'shelf'.

Chimney Buttress   55ft.   Hard Diff.
Start at the extreme north west corner. Climb a short slab and work left over easy ledges to the chimney. Cross the chimney and continue straight up the buttress. Finish to the left of the final jammed boulder in the chimney.

Heart Throb Crack   55ft.   Hard Severe (4b)
Start just left of the base of Highcliff Chimney. Climb into a niche by some awkward moves, after which the bottleneck is climbed to a ledge. The wedged block is passed on its right, regain the crack and climb direct to the top. A good route.

The Web   55ft.   E3 (5c)
Start as for Flake Crack. Climb this for 12ft. traverse right for a few moves until a mantleshelf can be made onto a ledge. Peg runner not in situ. Climb leftwards to the top.

Flake Crack   55ft.   V.S. (4c)   *
The obvious crack with the hanging flake in the back of the alcove. A good sustained pitch.

Cardiac Arrest   50ft.   E4 (6a)
Start a few feet left of Flake Crack at a slim scoop. Climb this move left at the top to the obvious ledge on the arete. Move back right to the centre of the wall and climb direct to the top. A long reach is helpful. On the only ascents so far preplaced runners have been put in Flake Crack.

Barnaby's Routes   15ft.   Hard Diff.
The prominent ledge at 15ft. can be reached by two routes, both need reversing as all the ways off are severe or above.

Rockhopper   55ft.   E2 (5b)
Start 3ft. right of Highcliffe Crack and climb the wall on small holds trending right to a ledge. Move right and climb the arete overlooking Cardiac Arrest on its lefthand side, to the top. A serious pitch.

Highcliffe Crack 60ft. Severe *
Start up the very prominent corner crack to the left of Barnaby's Routes. Climb the crackline all the way to the moor. A fine route.

Queer Street 70ft. Hard V.S. (4c) *
Start at a flake immediately left of Highcliffe Crack, climb the flake till standing on its summit. Pull on to the wall on the left and traverse beneath the overhang to a slim groove, follow this to the top.

Moonflower 35ft. E4 (6a) *
Immediately left of Queer Street is a blank wall. The route goes up this wall from the left to a blunt rib then straight up to join Queer Street. A serious route.

Moonflower Direct 35ft. E4 (6b)
Climb the blank wall direct.

Puffs Parade 40ft. Hard V.S. (5a)
Immediately right of a prominent crack line is an arete formed by the edge of the Moonflower slab. Climb the arete which is awkward to start. A long reach helps.

Scarecrow Crack 65ft. Hard V.S. (5a) **
The prominent crack. Climb the awkward crack by bold lay-backing to the security of a large ledge on the right. Continue up the awkward crack above to the summit blocks. A very fine route.

Stargazer 55ft. E3 (5c)
Follow Scarecrow Crack for 10ft. then hand traverse left for 10ft. Move up to the next break and climb the groove just right of the arete to the top. A good climb.

Stargazer Direct 55ft. E3 (6a)
Traverse out from under Scarecrow Crack and climb the wall direct. (there is a good runner in the final crack)

Desperate Dan E5 (6b)
Climb the wall direct.

Magic in The Air 55ft. E5 (6b) ***
Climb the arete right of Quasimodo.

Quasimodo 50ft. A2
Start 30ft. left of Scarcrow Crack at the base of a slab just left of a prominent arete. Climb the centre of the smooth wall (4 bolts, 3 pegs) to a small roof at 40ft. Move right and gain a line of bolts leading to the top.

HIGHCLIFFE NAB 21

Wombat   60ft.   Hard V.S. (5a)   *
Start as for Quasimodo. Climb the greasy slab to belay below the overhung corner. Ascend the impressive corner throughout on good holds in a superb position. A superb route.

Trampled Underfoot   80ft.   E1 (5b)
Follow Wombat for a few feet until it is possible to gain the obvious rightwards traverse line to the arete which is climbed by a wide crack.

Edge Hog   75ft.   Hard V.S. (5b)
Start just right of Damocles. Climb a shallow corner. Gain a hanging corner just left of the arete by an awkward move, continue steeply to a good hold. Climb the short but shattered wall above to a ledge beneath an overhanging corner. Climb the steep corner to the Moor.

Damocles   75ft.   V.S. (4b)
Start 20ft. left of Wombat about 15ft. higher up the slope. Easy ledges lead to an obvious undercut chimney. Climb the chimney until a bulge stops progress, a swing left is made to gain a protruding rib after which awkward moves lead to a grass ledge, (the climb can be finished here). Continue up a short wall then to a corner, climb over the obvious spike belay to the Moor.

Shield   30ft.   V.S. (4c)
Start 6ft. left of Damocles at a corner. Climb the corner to gain the wall above containing the shield. Climb the shield and the crack above.

The Split   20ft.   V. Diff.
Start 15ft. to the left of Damocles. Climb the strenous chimney throughout.

Equity   20ft.   Hard Diff.
Start 10ft. down the slope and 3ft. to the left of The Split at the base of a chimney. Climb the chimney throughout.

Twin Cracks   15ft.   Severe
Start 10ft. to the left of Equity. Climb the lichenous cracks to a final grassy scramble.

Ping   15ft.   Severe
Start beneath an overhang 10ft. to the left of Twin Cracks. Climb the obvious peg scarred crack moving right at the top. An awkward route especially if damp.

Greasy Chimney   20ft.   V. Diff.
The obvious chimney 15ft. to the left of Ping.

Cyclops 35ft. E3 (5c)
Left of Greasy Chimney is a large wall with an obvious eye in it. Climb this starting at the left arete passing the eye by moving right.

Slime Slab 35ft. Diff.
Start 20ft. left of Greasy Chimney. Climb the slab on chipped holds to a ledge. Belay, continue up the chimney above to grass ledges.

Sod Crack 30ft. Hard V.S. (5b)
The crooked corner just left of Slime Slab. Good cracks to start but an awkward finish on the right wall.

Skid Row 35ft. E1 (5b)
Climbs the slab right of Knuckle Duster. Start as for Knuckle Duster until a large foothold on the arete allows a step round onto the slab. Make some difficult moves up to some ledges. Finish leftwards. (Poor protection).

Knuckle Duster 35ft. Hard V.S. (5a)
Start in the corner 25ft. left of Slime Slab. Climb the corner to the right of Wee Dot, to the overhang, move right and climb the slab to the Moor above.

Wee Dot 30ft. Hard V.S. (5a)
Start in the same corner as Knuckle Duster. Climb the left hand of the two cracks until it is possible to mantleshelf onto a projection. Continue up the overhanging crack above. A fine route.

Up the Creek Without a Paddle 30ft. E2 (6a)
The obvious standing arete left of Wee Dot.

Sarcophecus 30ft. V.S. (4c)
Start in the large alcove left of Wee Dot. Climb the crack/groove in the right hand corner of the alcove.

Sunset Crack 30ft. Hard V.S. (5a)
The left hand corner of the alcove leads without difficulty to a ledge at half height. The wide overhanging crack above gives a difficult finish.

Queen Street 30ft. Hard V. Diff.
20ft. left of the alcove lies a slabby gardened crack. Climb the crack direct to the top. A good fine route.

Flange Crack 30ft. E2 (5c)
Climbs the awkward overhanging undercut curving crack 20ft. left of Queen Street. A fine hard route.

Green Crack　　20ft.　　V. Diff.
Start in a corner 10ft. to the left of Flange Crack. Climb the corner which is awkward to start.

Nice and Easy　　25ft.　　Hard Severe (4b)
Climbs the crack and slab 5ft. left of Green Crack (just right of Peeler).

Peeler　　30ft.　　E1 (5c)
Start beneath an overhang 12ft. left of Green Crack below an awkward peg scarred crack. Climb the crack and slab above. A fine route.

Gluon　　30ft.　　E2 (5c)
Climbs the arete immediately left of Peeler, joining Peeler to finish.

Cling on　　30ft.　　E2 (5c)
On the wall to the left of Gluon are two horizontal crack lines. Follow the lower peg scarred crack to the arete where it joins Peeler for the top slab.

Wanton　　20ft.　　Hard V.S. (5a)
Takes the horizontal crack at the top of the left wall of Peeler Buttress. Short but strenuous. Climb the horizontal crack to the arete, reach a horizontal crack and then the top.

On a small outcrop 100 yards left of Peeler are the following routes:

Lost Crack　　20ft.　　Severe
The prominent corner crack is climbed throughout.

Green Crack　　15ft.　　Severe
The thin bulging crack right of Lost Crack.

Green Wall　　20ft.　　Hard Severe (4b)
Starts up Green Crack then traverses right along an obvious line. Move up to finish.

Unnamed　　20ft.　　E2 (5c)
Climb the wall right of Holden's Wall.

Holden's Wall　　20ft.　　V.S. (4c)
To the left of Lost Crack is a prominent buttress. The climb starts to the left of the overhung prow. Climb the wall past a scoop to the edge of the prow on the right (good thread). Climb the prow direct, a fitting finish to a fine route.

Bullshitters Wall　　20ft.　　V.S. (5a)
Climbs the wall just left of Holdens Wall starting right of a block. Head for an obvious pocket, problematic.

The next three routes take the left wall of the prominent double roof buttress left of Holdens Wall.

Twister 15ft. Severe
Start below the prominent nose. Climb a few feet up the wall just right of a chimney until it is possible to step left and rejoin the chimney. Follow the chimney to the top.

Early Days 20ft. V.S. (4c)
Climb the obvious corner past a small overhang.

Be-Bop-Bap 20ft. V.S. (4c)
Start up Early Days then move right immediately. Continue just left of the cutaway.

Highcliffe Girdle 200ft. A2 V.S. (4c)
This traverse running from left to right starts at The Split. Climb this route until it is possible to traverse at a high level along the prominent fault rightwards. The traverse crosses Wombat, Scarecrow Crack, Highcliff Crack and Flake Crack to finish up Highcliff Chimney. The route involves some difficult free and artificial pitches. No description has been given as the line is obvious at a constant height. A fine expedition with good situations.

Easby Moor Area

On Easby Moor there lie numerous rock outcrops. The most important to the climber are the natural rock of Cook's Crag and the small quarry called Potter's Quarry. Climbs have also been recorded at Cockshaw Hill and Whetstone Nab.

HISTORY

The Barkers were once again the first to record climbs here, with ascents in the 1930's on Whetstone Nab and Potter's Quarry.

In the early 1960's G. Fixter and E. Marr between them climbed the majority of the routes at Cooks crags. A few harder routes have been added recently.

COCKSHAW HILL   G.R. 589107

This pleasant quarry has a fine situation and is quite picturesque with a pool in the main bay. Easily found on the northern spur of Easby Moor, it is best reached from Cribdale Gate where one can park near a cattlegrid. From here a track leads along the west of the moor and into the quarry.

Morning Wall   30ft.   A2
Starts in a small corner about 40ft. left of the pond. Climb the steep crack line and leave it by a difficult 'free' move to the right near the top. No belay.

The Boys are Back in Town   30ft.   E1 (5b)
The wall right of Morning Wall

The Problem   40ft.   Technically Hard V.S.
This is a traversing line which starts at the corner just to the left of the pond and traverses leftwards to join Morning Wall at the corner. The exposure is never more than 5ft. and the main difficulty lies in crossing a wide, smooth slab about 20ft. long on fragile holds. Entertaining if nothing else.

Divers Corner   35ft.   Mild Severe
Starts at the left-hand side of the pond. Gain horizontal ledges leading rightwards. Follow these to below a square cut corner. Climb the corner. No belays.

Divers Traverse 70ft. Diff.
Start as for Divers Corner but continue along the ledges rightwards to the main corner. Step across and down (awkward) onto the right wall and follow this at the lower level to the right bank of the pond. Pleasant as long as one remains on the rock.

Gribdale Buttress 30ft. Diff.
This is the rounded buttress just to the right of the pond. Climb a line of wandering ledges in the middle of the buttress. Care must be exercised when reaching the shale top. No belays.

WHETSTONE NAB G.R. 588103

Whetstone Nab lies on the north west spur of Easby Moor. It offers a range of routes in the easier grades but all are vegetated and have been thought unworthwhile for inclusion in this guide book.

POTTER'S QUARRY G.R. 589102

This crag lies just below Captain Cook's Monument on the summit of Easby Moor. It is approximately 200 yards W.N.W. from the monument.

The climbs are described from right to left.

First of Many 20ft. Hard V.S. (5b)
Ascends the wall at the right of the crag. Climb the bulge on pockets, ascend to the top with difficulty.

Square Corner Crack 20ft. Diff.
The corner left of the last climb.

Cook's Wall 20ft. Severe
Climb the wall left of the crack on small holds.

Cook's Rib 20ft. Diff.
The obvious ridge to the left of Cook's Wall. Ascend the ridge direct.

Endeavour 20ft. V. Diff.
Starts at foot of the last climb. Climb the wall leftwards to a ledge, climb diagonally rightwards to the top.

Resolution Corner 30ft. Hard Diff.
Start as for above. Gain a wide ledge running left to an exposed arete, make an awkward move into a sloping groove which leads easily to the top.

EASBY MOOR AREA

Direct Start 10ft. Severe
Start 12ft. left of above and ascend direct to the final groove.

Borboletta 20ft. E1 (5c)
Overhanging wall between Resolution Corner and Stretch.

Poison Letter E1 (5c)
Direct finish of Borboletta.

Stretch 20ft. V.S. (4c)
Now free. Climb the crack in the wall immediately right of the corner.

Zig Zag 20ft. V.S. (4c)
Start 5ft. left of the corner, ascend the crack to a poor finish.

Potter's Wall 20ft. V.S. (4c)
Start 5ft. left of Zig Zag. Climb a line of cracks and blocks almost to the top. Gain a ledge on the left.

Jumping Jack Flash 20ft. Hard V.S. (5a)
Ascend the overhung groove 6ft. left of Potter's Wall. Awkward start and groove.

G.B.G. 15ft. V.S. (5a)
Ascend the wall 6ft. left of Jumping Jack Flash, by an obvious pocket.

Friendly Gully 15ft. Mod.
The obvious gully left of G.B.G.

Friendly Ridge 15ft. Mod.
About 5ft. left of Friendly Gully a delicate series of steps.

Friendly Wall 10ft. Hard Severe (4b)
Climb leftwards across the wall from the foot of Friendly Ridge.

Tot 15ft. V. Diff.
Climb the corner 5ft. left of Friendly Ridge.

Flanged Wall 15ft. Hard Diff.
From Tot climb the wall on the left to another corner. Mantleshelf finish.

Direct Start 10ft. Severe
Climb the rounded nose of the corner on small holds.

About 150 yards right of Potter's Quarry is another small quarry. This is a good bouldering area attaining up to 12ft. in height.

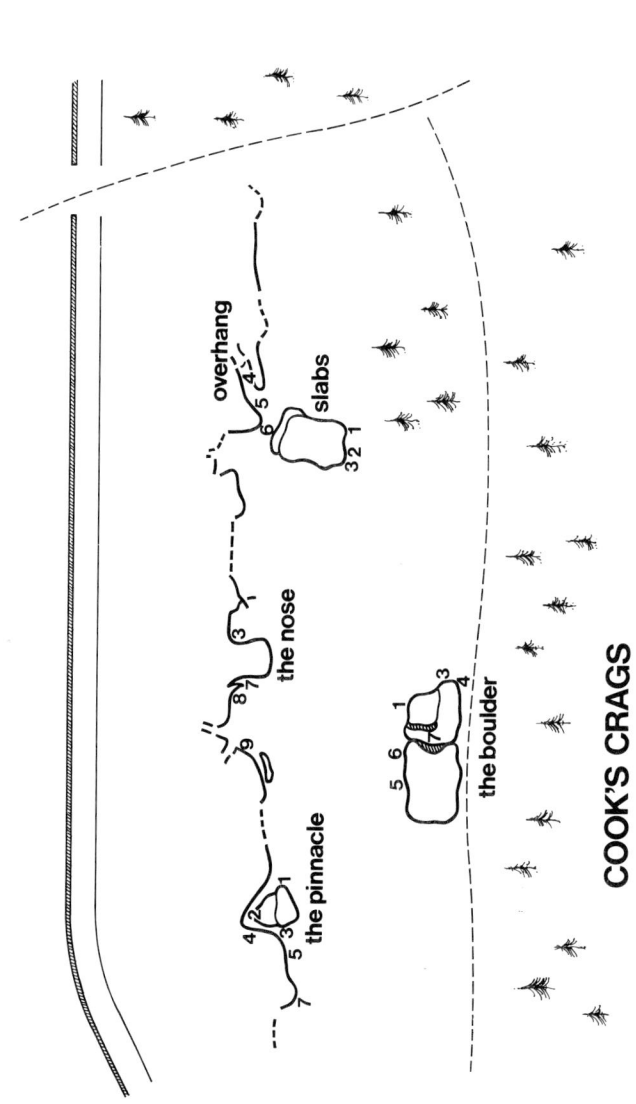

EASBY MOOR AREA

COOK'S CRAGS   G.R. 593097

These lie about 250 yards south of Captain Cook's Monument. Follow a broad path E.S.E. from the monument through a gateway in the wall and immediately turn right along an indistinct footpath.

The first group encountered is in the region of a large slab detached from the main crag, lying at an easy angle.

The climbs are described right to left.

THE SLAB AREA

1. The Slab - Right Edge   30ft.   Diff.
A pleasant route up the right-hand side.

2. The Slab - Centre   30ft.   V. Diff.
Start in a shallow depression in the middle of the slab. Climb the bulge direct and continue directly to the top.

3. The Slab - Left-hand   30ft.   Diff.
Climb the left-hand side of the slab. Awkward to start.

Above and a few feet right of The Slab is The Overhang.

4. Flake Wall   15ft.   V. Diff.
Climb the wall just to the left of a small gully.

5. Flanker   15ft.   V. Diff.
Climbs up right of the overhang passing a small flat ledge.

6. Stirrup   15ft.   Hard V.S. (5b)
This climbs the blunt nose of the overhang on poor rounded holds.

7. Brittle Band   15ft.   V. Diff.
A traverse of the overhang. Starts beneath the overhang crossing the steep wall to finish in the gully on the right.

About 100 yards left of The Slab is The Nose. The highest stand of rock on the crag.

THE NOSE AREA

1. Rufus   15ft.   Mod.
Start from a heather ledge below a projecting roof about 10 yards right of The Nose. Climb the slab and turn the roof on the left.

2. Endeavour   25ft.   V.S. (4c)
The wall right of Cook's Corner.

3. Cook's Corner   25ft.   V.S. (4c)
The obvious corner crack to the right of The Nose. Often wet and always unpleasant.

4. The Nose   25ft.   Hard V.S. (5b)
Start directly under The Nose. Climb the overhanging wall, moving left to a hole. Step left, then climb the arete, moving right onto a slab.

5. Sundancer   25ft.   E3 (5c)
Immediately left of The Nose is a line with a blind groove. Enter it from the left with difficulty and make awkward moves to the top.

6. Cookie   25ft.   Hard V.S. (5a)
Start 5ft. to the left of Sundancer. Climb direct to the top.

7. Two Tier Crack   20ft.   Hard V. Diff.
Well to the left of The Nose is a prominent flake crack splitting the face diagonally. Start below the crack in a shallow corner. Climb the awkward corner to finish up the cracks above.

8. The Corner   15ft.   Hard Severe (4b)
Climbs the smooth looking corner on the left-hand side of the flake described in 7.

9. Pobble Wall   15ft.   Severe
This is the sculptured wall separated from The Nose buttress by a divided gully. Climb the awkward wall a little left of the gully.

About 80 yards to the left of The Nose stands The Pinnacle, almost enclosed in a Vee shaped alcove.

PINNACLE AREA

Three climbs exist on The Pinnacle.

1. The Easy Way   15ft.   Diff.
Starts in the gully on the right of The Pinnacle. Climb the crack. This is normally used for descent.

2. The Pinnacle Nose   15ft.   V. Diff.
Starts in the back of the alcove. Climb the projection andcorner above.

3. The Other Way   15ft.   V.S. (4c) (strenuous)
On the left side of The Pinnacle climb the thin crack.

4. Greasy Wall   15ft.   Severe
The left wall of the Vee alcove. Start about 5ft. right of the arete and climb the wall on indifferent holds.

5. Deviation   15ft.   V.S. (4c)
Starts to the left of the alcove below two obvious holes in a groove. Gain the holes, then make a difficult step up and right to a ledge which is followed by a mantleshelf to the top.

6. Direct Finish   10ft.   Hard V.S (5a)
From the two holes, ascend direct to the top.

7. Easby Corner   15ft.   V.S. (4c)
The arete at the extreme left-hand end of the crag.

Below The Nose can be seen a huge split boulder. It is an excellent place for problems and included here are a few short routes. The most obvious feature is the wide chimney splitting the boulder. The climbs are described clockwise from this, starting on the side facing the crag.

1. Baldy   15ft.   V.S. (4c)
Start 10ft. left of the chimney at a sloping diagonal depression. Climb the bulge direct using obvious holes to the top.

2. Baldy's Traverse   15ft.   V.S. (4c)
Start as for Baldy but on reaching a horizontal crack a few feet up traverse left using the crack to finish by an awkward pull just to the left of the summit block.

3. The Boulder Direct   15ft.   V.S. (4c)
Start 5ft. right of the arete. Climb the steep wall direct to finish just left of the summit block.

4. The Boulder Ordinary   15ft.   V. Diff.
Gain the small ledge on the left of the arete then climb directly up the shallow vertical crack above.

5. Rampart   15ft.   V. Diff.
Start from a boulder 10ft. right of the chimney on the north side of the boulder. Step into a sloping crack on the wall. Follow it to a small corner and gain the slab above.

6. Green Slab   15ft.   Hard Severe (4b)
Start immediately right of the chimney at an undercut slab. Gain the slab and continue over the bulge to an awkward finish.

7. Chimney Variant   25ft.   Mild Severe
Starts 10ft. inside the chimney. Climb the left wall to the broad ledge. Climb the projecting nose of the leaning slab by some strenuous moves.

PARK NAB

Kildale

G.R. 611086

PARK NAB

This pleasant little outcrop lies at an elevation of about 900 feet south of Kildale village.

HISTORY

The standard easier routes at Park Nab were climbed by the Barker brothers and their friends in the 1930s. It was 25 years before J Hickman, N A Thompson, J Fletcher and A E Rout added more routes, showing what a fine job the pioneers had done.

In the mid sixties Johnny Adams was active here climbing Pessimist and Dynamo. In 1971 M Binks made the first free ascent of Dangle and a year later Chris Woodhall climbed the fine Pinnacle Face.

In the later 70s Nick Dixon added the notable Shere Khan after the removal of the offending bolts.

APPROACH

Take the Kildale road from Great Ayton or Stokesley. Turn sharp left 1½ miles after Easby village, pass under the railway and in ½ mile turn right on the minor road to Baysdale. After passing through the first gate park on the right and follow a path directly to the crag.

KILDALE FACE

1. Dangle   20ft.   Hard V.S. (5c)
Start at the left hand end of the crag, under a prominent roof. Climb up to the roof and then up to the top direct.

2. Lions Jaw   20ft.   Hard V.S. (5b)
Start about 10 feet right of Dangle in a corner below a wide crack. Ascend the corner followed by the crack.

3. Zero Route   15ft.   Hard V.S. (5a)
Round the corner to the right is a wall with a thin curving crack, climb this direct.

4. Cooks Gulley - Left Chimney   30ft.   Diff.
Ascend the chimney and buttress above.

5. Cooks Gulley - Table Climb   30ft.   Mod.
Start right of left chimney, climb the slabby wall and buttress above.

6. Castle Climb   35ft.   V. Diff.
(1) 20 feet. Climb wall just right of table, climb over a small bulge to a big ledge.
(2) 15 feet. Step off the outermost edge of the ledge and ascend the arete above.

7. The Keep   35ft.   V.S. (4c)
A series of variations on Castle Climb. Starts right of Castle Climb up a thin crack. Ascend onto the large ledge. Climb the wall left of Castle Climb to the top.

8. Grumble and Grunt   30ft.   Hard V.S. (5b)
Start in the alcove beneath the nose of Castle Climb. Climb the wide crack directly to the large ledge. Finish up The Keep.

HOLLY TREE WALL

9. Shere Khan   30ft.   E3 (5c)   *
Start beside a large boulder right of Grumble and Grunt. Ascend to two old bolt holes and move left to the arete. Move up this to the junction with Castle Climb, ascend this to the top. Hard and serious.

10. Styx   25ft.   Hard V.S. (5c)   *
Start as for Sherekhan, move right on small holds, then straight up the wall passing a large break. This route can be started off the boulder at 5b.

11. Twister   25ft.   E1 (5c)
The arete forming the left side of Twisting Chimney.

12. Twisting Chimney   25ft.   Diff.   *
The obvious chimney right of Styx.

13. Twin Cracks   20ft.   Severe   *
Start at the foot of the obvious twin cracks right of Twisting Chimney. Ascend these direct passing a holly tree. A fine route.

14. Dynamo   20ft.   Hard V.S. (5c)
Ascends the wall right of Twin Cracks with a hard mantleshelf at mid-height.

LADIES' GULLEY

15. Left Crack   20ft.   Diff.

16. Right Crack   20ft.   Severe
The crack immediately right of Left Crack.

KILDALE

THE PINNACLE

17. Pinnacle Crack - Left Hand 20ft. Diff.
The curving crack to the left of the Pinnacle.
Variation
The Wall to the left of this has been climbed at 5b.

18. Pinnacle Crack - Right Hand 20ft. V. Diff.
Start as for the left hand climb and pull out right into an overhanging crack.

19. Pinnacle Face 25ft. Hard V.S. (5c)
Start at the lowest point of the Pinnacle and climb the front face direct.

20. Chairman's Climb 25ft. V.S. (4b)
Start at a wide crack just right of Pinnacle Face. Ascend this and the almost vertical arete above to the top.

21. Chockstone Chimney 20ft. Diff.
The crack at the back of the Pinnacle.

JACK'S WALL

22. Wallbar Buttress 20ft. Hard V. Diff.
Climb the obvious twin cracks a few feet right of Chockstone Chimney.
Variation   Hard Severe (4b)
The undercut groove between Wallbar Buttress and Chockstone Chimney.

23. Picture This 20ft. Hard V.S. (5a)
Start just right of Wallbar Buttress below an obvious arete. Climb the wall and the arete above.

24. Scoop Chimney 20ft. Hard V. Diff.
The prominent gulley splitting Jacks Wall. Either of the two corners to finish.

25. Pessimist 20ft. E2 (5c)
Climb the arete right of Scoop Chimney throughout. A hard unprotected lead.

26. Hara-Kiri 25ft. Hard V.S. (5a)
Starts up the thin crack 3 feet right of Scoop Chimney, ascend this move right for 10 feet and ascend direct to top. A long reach is an advantage. A fine route.
Variation Finish   Hard V.S. (5b)
Climb the wall directly below the finish to gain the normal route at the end of the traverse.

27. Long Bow 20ft. Hard Severe (4b)
The prominent curving crack.

28. Bowstring 20ft. V.S. (5a)
The thin crack right of Long Bow which leads to the obvious cleft. Small holds.

29. The Bitter End 20ft. Hard V.S. (5b)
To the right of Bowstring is a letter box hold. Climb up to this and directly to the top.

30. The End 20ft. V.S. (5a)
The final arete of the crag direct.

31. The Girdle Traverse 180ft. V.S. (4c)
Start as for Dangle
    (1) Climb Dangle to the roof and hand traverse right past Lions Jaw and round the arete to Zero Route. Belay beneath Cooks Gulley left chimney.
    (2) Traverse right onto Cooks Gulley - Table Climb and move up to the Dining Table.
    (3) Move round the arete of Sherekhan and either hand traverse or foot traverse the break to Twisting Chimney. Belay.
    (4) Step round to Twin Cracks, awkward, and move across to left crack and maintain the same height to Pinnacle Crack - Left Hand.
    (5) Traverse round the Pinnacle and onto the ledge of Chairman's Climb. Move across Wallbar Buttress to belay in Scoop Chimney.
    (6) Move out of Scoop Chimney and into Hara-Kiri. Follow this till the crack of Long Bow can be gained. This is followed to the top or; one can move across into Bowstring and then follow The Bitter End and The End to the top. This automatically raises the standard to 5b Hard V.S.

The Girdle is a very fine route with beautiful climbing in excellent positions and should be treated with respect.

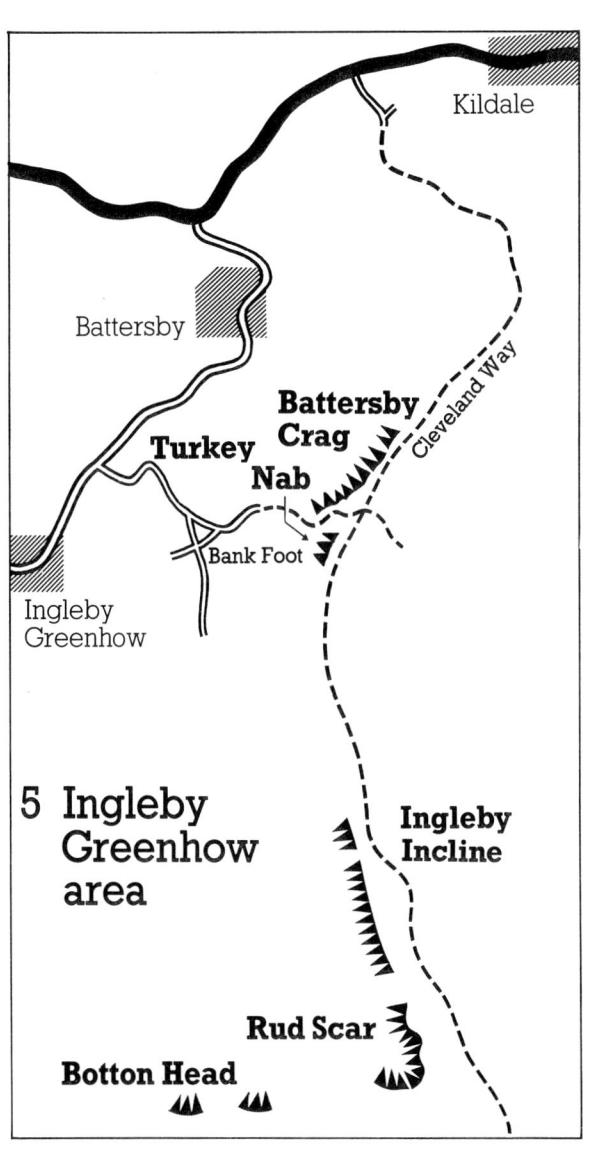

Ingleby Greenhow Area

At the time of writing there are longstanding access difficulties at the crags on the Grinkle Park Estate. The owners, Bass Limited, have refused to allow climbers on the Estate despite lengthy negotiations by the British Mountaineering Council.

The owners are particularly concerned that cars should not be taken on the moors, there should be no camping, and no fires.

Any climbers visiting the crags should take particular note of these concerns and should ensure that no damage or disturbance is caused that could give the owners reason for complaint.

BATTERSBY CRAG G.R. 602063

This is the name given to the long intermittent group of rocks on the North-West edge of Battersby Moor. It is easily reached from the brow of the old road running up to Turkey Nab, though of course there are many other approaches.

Foxes Lair   30ft.   Diff.
This climb is situated towards the left-hand end of the crags and lies almost directly behind Old Battersby. A deep chimney tucked into the left hand end corner of a buttress is climbed, followed by an easy traverse to the left and up a ridge.

Battersby Groove   25ft.   V.S. (4c)
To the right of Foxes Lair is an obvious groove. The route takes this throughout.

Fox Chase   25ft.   Hard V.S. (5b)
Climb the obvious groove on the opposite side of the buttress from Foxes Lair.

TURKEY NAB G.R. 598060

This well-known nab is situated about 1½ miles east of Ingleby Greenhow on Battersby Moor, just behind Bank Foot Farm. The climbs recorded are not on the nab proper but about 200 yards to the south of it. They are about 15 minutes walk from the Farm and, from the gateway leading onto the old Farndale road, are plainly visible near the top of the moors beyond. A track leading to the first climb on the left acts as a finger post.

Climbs are described from left to right.

INGLEBY GREENHOW AREA

Battersby Buttress 35ft. Severe
The first prominent buttress from the left of the rocks. Start at the foot of a vertical wall which is ascended on small holds to a narrow ledge. Continue up the slabs above to a large ledge and belays. Easy ledges above give access to the Moor.

Corner Direct 35ft. Hard Severe (4b)
Start at the arete right of Battersby Buttress. Ascend the arete direct to a ledge. Finish as for Oblique Crack or Battersby Buttress.

Batter Your Face 35ft. Hard V.S. (5a)
The wall and top groove to the right of Corner Direct.

Oblique Crack 35ft. Severe
Starts round the corner to the right of Battersby Buttress. Climb the parallel cracks by either jamming or laybacking to a stance. Continue up the final difficult corner crack.

Chicken Run 35ft. V.S. (4c)
Start 15ft. right of Oblique Crack. Climb the small corner to the overhang, step right, then climb to a ledge, belay.

Headline 35ft. Mild V.S. (4b)
The wall between Chicken Run and Diffman's Dilemma.

Diffman's Dilemma 35ft. Hard Severe (4b)
Climb the obvious arete a few feet right of Chicken Run.

Parallel Cracks *Left-hand* 35ft. V.S. (4c)
A few feet right of Diffman's Dilemma and around the corner are two obvious cracklines ending at a ledge. Climb the left hand line, moving left above the ledge.

Parallel Cracks *Right-hand* 35ft. Hard V.S. (5b)
Climb the right-hand crackline.

Extra 30ft. V.S. (4c)
Climb the wall right of Right-hand Parallel Crack.

INGLEBY INCLINE G.R. 604039

This crag, several hundred yards long, lies on the western edge of Greenhow and Ingleby moors overlooking the old railway incline. It is best reached by taking the Battersby road out of Ingleby Greenhow, and the first turning right to Bankfoot Farm. At the farm take the cinder track to the right and proceed for 1½ miles to some cottages. Continue through the gate and up the incline to the limit of the forest where the first buttress can be seen directly up the hillside on the left. This may be approached directly or by gaining the cutting near the top of the Incline and following the escarpment back to the crag. The latter will be easier when the bracken is high.
Climbs are described from right to left.

AMERICAN BUTTRESS

Fifteen Love 15ft. V. Diff.
This lies 9ft. right of the next climb.

Seven Up 15ft. Diff.
The right most of the two chimneys.

Crack and Up 15ft. Diff.
The easy chimney on the left side of the buttress.

30 yards left of this is a buttress split on its left side by two prominent cracks.

POLITICAL BUTTRESS

Problems 15ft. Diff.
The right crack.

Communist Crack 15ft. Diff.
The left crack.

60 yards to the left lies

MACS BUTTRESS

Pizza Pie 15ft. Diff.
Climbs the obvious chimney with a holly tree in its left wall.

Heather Crack 20ft. Severe
Left of Pizza Pie is a thin, heather filled crack. Climb this throughout.

Hash Browns 20ft. V.S. (4c)
Left of Heather Crack is a small corner. This is climbed to a difficult mantleshelf at the top.

INGLEBY GREENHOW AREA 11

Big Mac   20ft.   V. Diff.
Climb the slab 15ft. left of Hash Browns.

The next buttress is 100 yards to the left and has the word FOX HUNTERS carved in the rock at the back of a small cave at its base.

HUNTERS BUTTRESS

Chock Crack   15ft.   V.S. (4c)
The clean jamming crack in the corner towards the right hand end of the buttress.

Marakesh Express   15ft.   Hard Severe
Climb the front of the buttress just left of Chock Crack

Corner Crack   15ft.   Severe
Climb the crack left of Chock Crack to an awkward finish.

Block Chimney   20ft.   Severe
12ft. left of Corner Crack. Climb over awkward jammed block and scramble through holly up the chimney above.

Pickpocket   25ft.   Severe
Climb the front of the buttress 12ft. left of block chimney.

Rack and Pinion   25ft.   Severe
Just left of Pickpocket. Gain a curving ledge and climb it rightwards to a ridge. Mantleshelf onto a ledge and climb to the top.

Hunters Chimney   20ft.   Hard V. Diff.
Start in the cave at the left end of the buttress and climb the chimney. Awkward to start.

40 yards left the next buttress is

CLEFT BUTTRESS

Easter   15ft.   Mod.
The obvious crack at the right hand end.

Brutus   20ft.   Hard V.S. (5b)
The wall between Easter and Pobble Wall.

Pobble Wall   20ft.   V.S. (4c)
The sculptured wall 12ft. left of Easter.

The Corner   20ft.   V.S. (4c)
The obvious curving corner crack at the left end of Pobble Wall. Harder than it looks.

40 yards left of Cleft Buttress is a large boulder.

I Surrender   15ft.   Diff.
The arete on the left side of the boulder.

7 yards left is a small outcrop.

Babelogne   20ft.   Hard Severe
From the bottom of the slab climb left onto the arete and then trend right to the top. Very entertaining.

30 yards left is an easy slab.

Pigs on the Wing   15ft.   Diff.
Ascend the centre of the slab.

50 yards left is a large buttress with a perched block on top.

CAPSTONE BUTTRESS

Sloopy   45ft.   V.S. (4c)
Start below a 'V' groove 10ft. right of the overhang. Climb the wall and pass a shelf to reach the 'V' groove. Ascend the groove and slabby wall above.

Ceasor   45ft.   Hard V.S. (5a)
Climb up the right hand end of the overhang to the lip, traverse left for 6ft. then continue to the top.

Modern Primitive   45ft.   E3 (5b)   *
This route starts beneath the overhang at its widest point. Climb up to the roof, climb the roof at a crack to gain the ledge above. Step right and continue up the front of the buttress.

Black Crack   25ft.   Severe
Starts in a large corner to the left of Modern Primitive. Climb the crack throughout.

Dreams   25ft.   V. Diff.
To the left of Black Crack. Climb the arete to a ledge and continue to the top.

The Chain   15ft.   Diff.
Climb the twin crack left of Dreams.

Holly Wall   20ft.   V. Diff.
Climb the wall 20ft. left of The Chain.

INGLEBY GREENHOW AREA   43

Holly Crack   20ft.   Diff.
The crack forming the left edge of Holly Wall.

The Cleft   15ft.   Diff.
The obvious corner just left of Holly Crack.

Swinger   20ft.   Severe
15ft. left of The Cleft. Climb the right hand side of the arete.

Twister   15ft.   Severe
Starts in a corner 15ft. right of the extreme left end of the rocks. Climb the crack throughout.

The next buttress is 120 yards left.

ROWAN BUTTRESS

Wall and Slab   25ft.   V.S. (5a)
Climbs the wall and slab at the right hand end of the buttress.

Crack and Groove   30ft.   Severe
Starts 15ft. left of Wall and Slab. Climb the thin crack and the right hand groove above. Very pleasant.

Wall and Groove   30ft.   V.S. (4c)
10ft. left of Crack and Groove. Climb the delicate wall to the heather ledge. Finish up the left hand groove.

Next Crack   20ft.   Diff.
10ft. left of Wall and Groove.

Twin Cracks   15ft.   Diff.
Starts 10ft. right of the extreme left end of the rocks. Climb the cracks. N.B. Rowan tree in left crack.

80 yards left lies

Puffing Billy   20ft.   Severe
The obvious thin crack at the left end of the rocks.

Choo Choo   25ft.   Diff.
30ft. left of Puffing Billy across a gully. Climb the bulge on rounded holds.

Jet Lag 15ft. Mod.
The easy chimney 22 yards left of Choo Choo.

Dangle 15ft. Hard V.S. (5a)
Climb, on difficult jams, the crack in the overhang 14 yards left of Jet Lag.

Chatanooga 20ft. V. Diff.
Starts beneath an overhang on a small buttress 20 yards left of Dangle. Keep left to the skyline then up to the top.

GREENHOW BUTTRESS

Smoothy 20ft. Severe
Faces Chatanooga across an open gully. Climb the rounded wall direct to finish left of a prominent summit block.

A Question of Sport 20ft. Hard V.S. (5b)
Starts 15ft. left of Smoothy, just right of a small overhang. Climb the shallow scoop to a break, step right and continue up the centre of the slab.

A Matter of Taste 20ft. Hard V.S. (5a)
Start as for A Question of Sport. Climb up to the break, step left and finish up the slab.

Signal Ridge 35ft. Hard V. Diff.
15ft. left of A Matter of Taste. Start just left of the lowest point. The middle section is climbed on its left face. Continue up the edge to the top.

Saunter Slab 35ft. Mild V.S. (4b)
Climb the centre of the slab 10ft. left of Signal Ridge.

Cosy Corner 35ft. V. Diff. *
Start under the large overhang. Climb the short corner to a ledge. Continue up the corner to the moor. The classic of the crag.

Time Captain 35ft. E3 (5c) *
Start a few feet left of Cosy Corner at a rightward facing corner. Climb the corner and short wall above to an obvious crack leading rightwards to beneath the large roof. At the roof traverse left round the overhang and gain the slab above by a hard move. Climb direct to the top. Further hard moves.

Ellis's Eliminate 35ft. E3 (5c)
Start up the outside of Greenhow Chimney. On the right wall is a horizontal ledge. Hand traverse the ledge until it runs out, make hard moves to gain a groove and finish more easily.

Greenhow Chimney   25ft.   Diff.
Start 30ft. left of Cosy Corner. Climb the chimney. Very entertaining.

Little Chimney   15ft.   Diff.
Starts round the left flank of the buttress well up the hillside.

The overhang has been ascended on bolts at A2 V.S.
The buttress also has a low level traverse technically 5b.

200 yards left is

SOUTH BUTTRESS

Slipstream   15ft.   V. Diff.
The obvious flake crack on the right side of the buttress

South Buttress Direct   30ft.   Hard V.S. (5c)
Start at the centre of the buttress. Climb onto the ledge, then move up the front of the buttress using the upside down flake. Move round to the right to a spike, then up on sloping holds to finish. The route is very strenuous but well protected.

The last significant outcrop is

NORTH BUTTRESS

Parallels   15ft.   Severe
The crack on the right side of the buttress.

Clarity   30ft.   Hard V.S. (5b)
Starts to the left of centre of the buttress. Climb the slab, move right off the slab onto the bulging rock, then climb the front of the buttress.

Time   30ft.   Severe
Starts as for Clarity. From the slab continue up the jamming crack above.

NOTE - 30 yards right of South Buttress and lower down there is a minor outcrop called CELLAR WALL. Several short routes can be devised here.

RUD SCAR G.R. 606025 - 604022

Follow the route to Ingleby Incline and ascend the incline as far as the cutting. Rud Scar lies a few hundred yards across the moors to the right. It is comprised of two separate outcrops, referred to as East Band and West Band.

EAST BAND

This is the first band of rocks to be reached from the above approach. The climbs are described from left to right and the first route starts 5ft. left of the prominent corner.

The Scoop 20ft. Diff.
Climb to the left of the scoop by a crack to a ledge. Step into the scoop which is climbed to the top.

Ginger 20ft. Hard V. Diff.
5ft. right of The Scoop is a prominent corner. Climb this throughout to a large tree. Awkward start.

Hosted's Horror 25ft. V.S. (4c)
25ft. right of Ginger. The steep crack is climbed to an awkward finish.

Roraima 40ft. Severe
Start 20ft. right of Hosted's Horror at a large flake below some trees. Climb the wall left of the flake to the trees. Belay. Climb awkwardly over the overhang and finish diagonally right up the wall.

Twenty yards right of Roraima at the extreme end of the buttress and further up the slope is

Truant 15ft. Diff.
Climb the corner.

The next buttress is 25 yards further on. Some bouldering has been done on the buttresses between.

Tapestry 50ft. Hard Severe (4b)
Start just right of a wet gully at a sharp flake crack. Climb the crack to a ledge, move left and ascend the wall to a ledge. Continue up the corner crack above on jammed blocks.

Smackwater Jack 50ft. Mild V.S. (4c)
Start 10ft. right of Tapestry. Climb the corner mainly on the left wall to a ledge. Move right and up for a few feet, then traverse leftwards to a groove. Finish as for Tapestry.

INGLEBY GREENHOW AREA

20 yards further right is

Daddy Long Legs 30ft. V.S. (4c)
Ascend the steep corner and overhang on the left of the buttress pulling into a groove on the right near the top.

Speechless 30ft. Mild V.S. (4c)
Climb up to the tiny cave. Ascend the overhang into a groove joining Daddy Long Legs.

15 yards right is a small buttress

North Sea Gas 25ft. V. Diff.
Climb the ledges at the left of the buttress, passing a small tree and finishing up a flake.

Ekofisk 25ft. Severe
Start 20ft. right of North Sea Gas. Climb steeply to a small tree. Finish up an awkward corner above.

35 yards further right is the largest continuous buttress.

.303 30ft. V. Diff.
Climb the corner to a large block. Surmount this and finish up a loose groove. Not worthwhile.

Old Friends 40ft. Mild V.S. (4b)
Climb the corner crack 10ft. right of .303. A good climb.

Punky's Dilemma 40ft. V.S. (4c)
Start 10ft. right of Old Friends. Climb the wall right of shattered ledges. The groove is awkward.

15ft. further right are two small corners halfway up the crag

Fakin' It 35ft. Severe
Climb the wall to the first ledge. Ascend the left wall with difficulty. Finish up the crack above.

Overs 35ft. Diff.
Climb the wall to the first ledge 5ft. right of Fakin' It. Ascend the right hand corner to large holds.

Above this buttress is another tier of rock up to 25ft. high. Some climbs have been done here at an easy grade but there is scope for development at all grades.

WEST BAND

An attractive group of rocks about 250 yards beyond the East Band across a large grassy depression.

Shepherd's Slab   30ft.   Diff.
Starts at the foot of a broad slab, at the left of the band. Climb the slab to a heathery ledge. Finish up a short wall above, near its left end.

Shepherd's Buttress   25ft.   V.S. (4c)
Start 15ft. right of Shepherd's Slab. Climb the buttress to a good ledge then up the face above keeping slightly to the left.

Herdwick Wall   30ft.   Severe
Lies around the corner 20ft. right of Shepherd's Buttress. Climb the middle of the wall to the overhang. Step right and climb until one can step back left onto the face and climb directly to the top.

Merino Corner   30ft.   Diff.
Start 10ft. right of Herdwick Wall. Climb to a holly tree and up the crack just behind it.

Flake Crack   25ft.   Hard V. Diff.
The crack just right of Merino Corner.

Shadrach   40ft.   Severe
Start 20ft. right of Flake Crack. Gain a shallow niche and climb diagonally leftwards to a sloping ledge. Traverse left to Flake Crack and finish up this.

Y Crack   30ft.   Severe
Start as for Shadrach. Follows the obvious crack to a holly, continue up to the short corner above.

Meshach   30ft.   Severe
Start 12ft. right of Shadrach at the foot of a steep brown slab. Climb the slab to a holly, finish up the corner above.

Meshach Variation Finish   40ft.   V.S. (4c)
Start as for Meshach. Climb the slab a few feet then trend rightwards to the corner of the buttress. Ascend the overlap to the top. A good route.

Abednego   30ft.   Severe
Start 10ft. right of Meshach at the foot of a crack. Climb the crack to a ledge, continue up a sharp edge to a second ledge. Traverse into the chimney and climb the left wall direct.

Hawk Chimney   20ft.   Diff.
The chimney with a chockstone just right of Abednego.

INGLEBY GREENHOW AREA

BOTTON HEAD G.R. 592019

These rocks lie on the northern edge of Urra Moor, overlooking Greenhow Botton. A few minutes to the south-east of the rocks stands the trig point which marks the summit of the moor and the highest point in Cleveland.

HISTORY

The Headmaster and pupils of Ayton Friends' School were responsible for the easier climbs on this crag.

APPROACH

The rocks can be reached in a variety of ways, but the most pleasant and least arduous starts from the Bilsdale side of the top of Clay Bank. Pass through Hagg Gate at the end of the stone wall, and follow a track which runs first east and then veers to the south-east along Carr Ridge (Lyke Wake Walk). In ¾ mile the rocks of Botton Head can be seen in front and slightly to the left. A further plod through the heather, where the track becomes less distinct, leads to the top of the rocks, which comprise three bands. Band III is the nearest to Clay Bank and Band I nearest to Ingleby Incline.

The climbs on each band are described from left to right.

BAND I

The bay of rock nearest to Ingleby Incline.

Swathmore Crack 25ft. Mod.
Starts 25ft. from the left of the rocks. Ascend a corner and crack and then broken rocks to the top.

Screwy 25ft. V. Diff.
Start just right of the last route underneath a projection. Climb diagonally right to a platform. Follow the chimney above.

Firbank Chimney 25ft. Mod.
Start 10ft. right of Screwy. Follow the chimney throughout.

Band I Eliminate 15ft. Severe
Start 20 yards to the right of the last route beneath an undercut crack. Climb this. Awkward to start.

Late Out 20ft. V. Diff.
Start 30ft. right of Band I Eliminate beneath an ash. Mount a buttress on good holds which leads to a short but strenuous crack. Finish on the right.

Long Stop 25ft. V. Diff.
Start 30ft. right of Late Out, at the right edge of a grassy rake. Slabs lead diagonally right. Leave these as soon as possible and climb direct to the top.

Maiden Over 30ft. Diff.
Start as for Long Stop. Follow the slabs diagonally right to a ledge. Descend below a small overhang and finish up a crack to the right.

Splits 15ft. Severe
Start 15ft. right of Long Stop. Climb the groove and short crack above.

BAND II

This is the middle bay.

Band II Eliminate 20ft. V.S. (4c)
Start 25ft. right of the first rocks. Climb the undercut crack to a small tree where an exit to the right is made.

The Cleft 20ft. Hard V. Diff.
Start 6ft. right of the last climb. Climb the cleft to a grass recess. Finish up the right wall.

Parallel Cracks 25ft. V.S. (4c)
Start 12ft. right of The Cleft. Climb the steep cracks to a grassy scramble.

Dido 15ft. V. Diff.
Start 15ft. to the right of the last climb and at a higher level. Just right of a cave. Easy rocks lead to the foot of a short but steep cleft on the left, which is climbed.

Aeneas 25ft. Diff.
Start 5ft. to the right of Dido but rather lower down. Climb an awkward rib for 10ft. and then climb either the right or left face of the buttress above.

Boss Chimney 35ft. Hard V. Diff.
Start 30ft. to the right of Aeneas, round a small buttress. Climb a corner to a terrace. Gain and climb the chimney above.

En route to Band III which lies 150 yards right of Band II one passes some isolated rocks. One climb has been made here:

Nogo 15ft. V.S. (4c)
Starts in a corner immediately right of the first corner. Climb the crack with difficulty to an awkward finish.

BAND III

A prominent feature of this band is a large slab embedded in the hollow at the foot of the crag.

Quakers Oats   15ft.   Hard Diff.
Start 20ft. to the left of the slab. Climb the steep crack on good holds. Pleasant.

Quakers Way   35ft.   Hard Severe (4b)
Start just right of the last climb. Traverse right for 10ft. just above the ground to a crack. Climb the crack step right and climb a second crack to a stance. Continue straight up to the top. A good route.

Skipjack   35ft.   Diff.
Start from the foot of the slab. Climb the right edge of the slab to a corner of jumbled blocks. Move up on the left and out onto a small, exposed ledge. A large ledge above leads to the moor.

Ruddigore   20ft.   Mod.
Start to the right of the slab but much further up the slope in a corner. Climb the crack and chimney above.

Geordies Delight   35ft.   Hard Diff.
Start 20ft. right of the slab at the foot of the wall. Climb the middle of the wall to the foot of a groove. Follow the groove to the top.

Angels Tread   35ft.   Severe
Start to the right of the last climb, but left of the nose of the buttress. Step on the wall and climb direct to a ledge. The climbing above the ledge is harder and exposed.

Band III Eliminate   25ft.   Hard V.S. (5a)
Start below a smooth groove 20ft. right of Angels Tread and right of the nose. Climb the groove with difficulty to finish over some doubtful blocks. Traverse left and finish up the corner. Interesting.

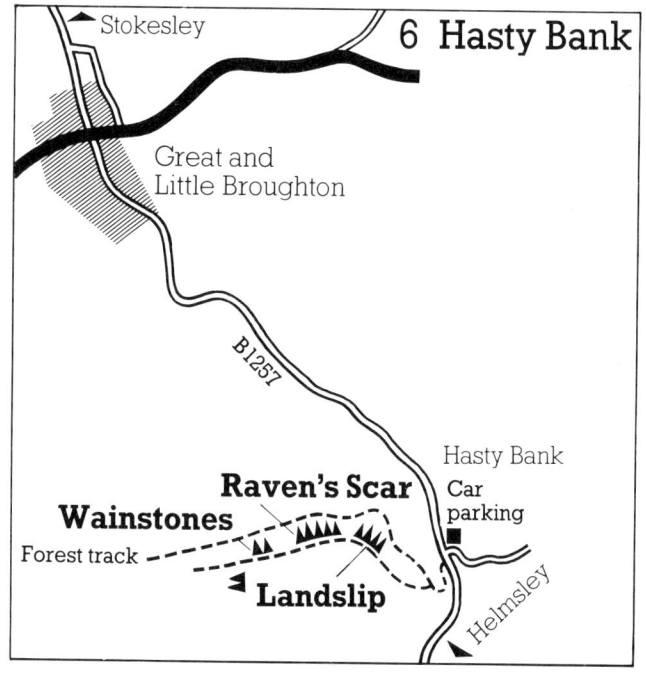

Hasty Bank Area

LANDSLIP G.R. 567038

Landslip is the band of rocks which flanks the east end of Hasty Bank and can easily be seen from the summit of Clay Bank. Unfortunately most of the climbing in the main area is either dangerous or unpleasant due to the effects of land subsidence.

HASTY BANK AREA

APPROACHES
The crags can be quickly reached from the car park near the summit of Clay Bank. Take the path that skirts the north-east flank of Hasty Bank above the tree line. In about ⅛ mile scramble up to the crags on the left.

At the extreme right hand end of the crag (Ravenscar can be seen from here) is a sound buttress about 20ft. high. The climbs are described from right to left on the face of the buttress overlooking the car park.

Spring Crack 15ft. V. Diff.
The obvious corner crack is climbed on good hand jams.

The Gash 15ft. V.S. (5a)
Climbs the obvious gash 5ft. left of Spring Crack.

White Hill Face 25ft. V. Diff.
Starts at the toe of the buttress. Climb left for a few feet and then continue directly up the face above.

Alternative start
Traverse up and left on to the face from the foot of the gash.

Heather Brae 20ft. Diff.
Start 6ft. left of the toe of the buttress at a short corner crack. Climb the crack and groove, finishing up a crack on the left.
Some 30 yards. left of these routes is a slabby buttress.

Red Grouse 30ft. Hard Severe
Follows the flake and green corner crack.

Well to the left the highest and most prominent buttress on Landslip (lying left of centre) has two faces either side of an arete with a square overhang at third height.

No Expectations 30ft. E4 (6b)
The obvious blind flake right of the arete (2 peg runners).

Fame 25ft. E3 (6a) *
Climbs the wall on the left of the arete. Start in a corner, move right and then back left.

HASTY BANK AREA

RAVEN'S SCAR G.R. 566037

This crag is situated on the north side of Hasty Bank overlooking the Vale of Cleveland. Ravenscar is one of the major sandstone cliffs in Cleveland, particularly for climbers looking for routes in the middle and upper grades. Its popularity does not reflect this mainly because the crag is north facing, is mossy in appearance, and can take a couple of days to dry after heavy rain. However, the crag appears greener than it really is, and the rock is generally clean. In general the climbs are well protected, follow steep natural lines, and tend to be rather strenuous.

HISTORY

The first climbers to visit Raven's Scar were C.E. and D. Burrow and party in 1912-13. C.S. and T.H. Tilly were also there in 1932. However, possibly owing to the northerly aspect of the crag and its vegetated appearance Ravenscar seems to have been little frequented until 1954 and 1955. In those years members of the Cleveland Mountaineering Club excavated the crag and R.B. Whardell eventually unearthed and climbed Tumble Down Dick, Dirty Dick, Sunshine Slab and paved the way for R.A. Chester to ascend the Waterslide. About the same time J. Hickman climbed the tough Ahab and in the latter part of the '50's T. Sullivan and W.J. Dell added the awkward Harlot's Groove together with the steep artificial climbs Satchmo and Ella.

Other routes were aid climbed but the subsequent change in attitudes and improved protection techniques lead to those routes being attempted free. Of particular note were Tony Marr's first free ascent of Satchmo in 1970, followed by John Redhead and Chris Shorter's free ascent of Ella in the mid-70's. The former is an undisputed classic and the latter one of the hardest and most impressive routes in the area.

About the same time John Redhead and Chris Shorter also added the technical Screwy and fine Fever Pitch. More recently Paul Ingham freed Pencil Line and added the new route Hooker.

APPROACHES

The best approach is from the car park near the summit of Clay Bank, about 2 miles from Great Broughton on the Stokesley to Helmsley road. As for Landslip take the forestry path which skirts the north-east flank of Hasty Bank above the tree line. The path rises steeply at first while heading south-west, but levels off as the path turns towards the west. At this point the crag can be seen above on the left and access is by means of a stile below the highest point of the crag.

RAVEN'S SCAR

THE CLIMBS

1. Thrasher   35ft.   V.S. (4b)
Starts about 15 yds. right of the lefthand end of the cliff below a shallow niche in the overhang. Pull over the roof into the niche and exit awkwardly on to the grass ledge. Climb up right to finish.

2. Suede Shoe Shuffle   35ft.   Hard V.S. (5c)
10ft. right of Thrasher is another break in the same overhang. Climb the break with difficulty, followed by the slabby nose above.

3. En Passant   35ft.   Severe
Starts up the prominent corner to the right of the previous climbs. Follow the corner to a ledge and climb the crack above.

4. Lazy Bones   35ft.   Hard Severe (4a)
Just to the right of En Passant is another corner which faces it. Climb the crack in the corner of the slab to its top where a difficult move left leads to a ledge. Climb the corner above to the top.

5. Afterthought   35ft.   Hard V.S. (4c)
Start just left of Lazy Bones. Climb the centre of the slab. Finish up the left arete. Rather contrived.

6. Grooves-ology   35ft.   V.S. (4c)   *
Start up the corner crack of Lazy Bones but instead of moving left make a semi-layback move on to a ledge on the right. The layback cracks above are climbed to the top. A good climb.

7. Stardust   35ft.   E1 (5b)   *
About 6ft. right of Lazy Bones is a flake crack. Climb up the crack and short wall above on to the ledge of Grooves-ology. Climb the pegged scarred crack on the right to the top.

8. Screwy   45ft.   E4 (6b)   *
Starts just right of Stardust at a crack. Climb up this then very thin moves allow the ledge to be reached. Move left then right on to a higher ledge. Pull over the bulge on to the face above. Traverse left around the arete (runner in Stardust) and follow the overhanging arete above to the top. Artificial but technical and bold.

8a. Screwy (right-hand finish)   E3 (6a)
From the higher ledge climb the wall rightwards to join Satchmo.

9. Satchmo   45ft.   E1 (5b)   ***
Climb the obvious overhanging corner right of Screwy. A well protected classic and a fine climb.

HASTY BANK AREA 57

10. Stratagem   40ft.   E4 (6b)   **
The old aid route Ella. Starts on the platform 10ft. right of Satchmo. Climb over the bulge and climb the thin crack to ledges (thread). Follow the slanting crack above (peg runner in situ). Fine climbing with subtle difficulties.

11. Appache Roof   E3 (5c)
The roof to the right of Stratagem gives an amusing problem.

A gully now splits the cliff but does not make a very good descent.

12. Sunshine Slab   30ft.   Diff.
Starts at the bottom of the gully. Follow ledges up left then the final slabby corner.

To the right of the gully is a fine overhanging wall with a corner at its right hand end.

13. Too Young to Fly   30ft.   Hard V.S. (5a)
Starts just to the right of the left hand end of the wall. Reach a horizontal slot, jump for the break and continue to the ledge (belay). Climb the slab via a crack on the right (surprisingly difficult).

14. Rock Bottom   40ft.   E3 (6b)
Above the Ahab hand traverse is a horizontal 'pea pod'. Utilising the hand traverse ledge mantleshelf and reach the pod. Move slightly right to a horizontal slot (runner). Reach for the next break and continue to the belay ledge. Pass the bulge at a large protruding hold, and so to the top. Belay well back.

15. Ahab   40ft.   Severe (4b)   *
About halfway along the wall a hand traverse line runs into the corner on the right. Follow this, then up the corner to a ledge. Climb the crack to a precarious perched block on the top.

15a. Ahab (direct start)   15ft.   Hard V.S. (5c)
The problematic groove.

16. Jonah   15ft.   Hard V.S. (5a)
To the right of Ahab is a cave formed by jutting overhangs. Gain the groove which splits the roof by a spectacular layback move. Climb up to join Ahab.

17. Moby Dick   40ft.   Hard Severe (4a)
Starts in the sandy gully to the right of the cave. Traverse out left above the overhangs, then diagonally right to the large ledge. Climb the delicate nose above to finish over the perched block.

The following climbs are to the right of the sandy gully on the tallest part of the cliff.

18. Dirty Dick   50ft.   Diff.
As clean as its name implies. Start about 10 yds. to the left of the lowest part of the cliff at a groove below a canopy. Follow this to a ledge at 10ft. Traverse left, then diagonally left past a bulge. Climb the final corner crack.

19. Forest Face   65ft.   Hard Severe (4b)   **
Start as for Dirty Dick, climb diagonally left for 20ft. to a broad ledge. Traverse right along this ledge to a short groove in an exposed position above the canopy. Climb this (crux) then move right to an easier crack. Follow the crack then chimney above (Lion's Mouth) to the top - a fine open climb.

20. Red Light   40ft.   Hard V.S. (5a)
Start directly below the thin crack to the left of the Forest Face crux. Climb the short rightwards facing corners to a ledge. Continue up the thin crack to another ledge. Finish up the arete on the right.

A route slightly to the left of Red Light can be climbed at a similar grade.

21. Forest Face Direct   50ft.   E1 (5c)
A bold direct start to Forest Face. Start directly below the crux groove of Forest Face. Climb up and mantleshelf over the first overhang, pass the canopy towards its right hand end, and join Forest Face by an awkward mantleshelf. Continue over the top overhang.

22. Hooker   50ft.   E1 (5b)   *
Climbs the wall left of Harlot's Groove. Starts up a thin crack in a slab to a break. From the break climb up to reach an obvious pocket below the block and continue to the ledge. Climb the wall and the small overlap to the top.

23. Harlots Groove   55ft.   V.S. (4c)   *
Start just to the left of an open chimney (Tumble down Dick) that defines the right hand side of the face. Climb the wall to the roof. Move left with difficulty to the groove. Climb this and the slab above to a ledge. Climb the inverted 'V' scoop and the slab to the top.

24. Harlots Groove Variation   Hard V.S. (5b)
Instead of climbing the groove, climb, via a prominent jug, the overhang to the right on to a slabby wall. Climb up this to the belay ledge.

HASTY BANK AREA

25. Tumble Down Dick. 85ft. Diff. *

An excellent climb for beginners. Start at the lowest point of the cliff. Follow the open chimney to a large platform. Climb the blocks on the left and up a short corner to the moor.

26. Tumble Down Crack 50ft. Severe

A poor first pitch. Start 30ft. right of the last climb. Climb up easy ledges to an open corner and follow this to the large ledge of Tumble Down Dick. Ascend the overhanging groove above. Traverse right and up to the top.

26a. Alternative Start Hard Severe (4b)

A better first pitch to Tumble Down Crack. Climb the thin corner crack to the right of the normal start.

27. The Omen 50ft. Hard V.S. (5b)

Start up the variation start to Tumble Down Crack until it is possible to swing out right on two large square jugs. Follow the overhanging tower above to the top. Gymnastic but well protected.

28. Omen Arete 40ft. E1 (5b)

Start up The Omen then traverse to the arete. Make a hard move to stand on the sloping ledge on the right wall. Continue up the arete to the top.

29. Waterslide 55ft. Hard Severe (4a) *

This climbs the green chimney to the right of the last climb. Climb the wall into the chimney and follow this to the top. A more interesting finish can be made by traversing into the twin cracks in the wall on the right.

30. Fever Pitch 55ft. E2 (5b) **

Start up the groove to the right of Waterslide, and follow it to a bulge. Move up right to a horizontal crack. Climb up the blunt arete on the left to a resting place and then climb the thin crack above. Bold and fine.

31. Gangrene 55ft. E3 (6b)

Climb the juggy overhanging wall to the right of the initial groove of Fever Pitch moving slightly left to the bulge, and up to a pre-placed peg runner (not in situ). Mantleshelf with difficulty, move right then more easily up the arete.

32. Via Anna 35ft. Hard Severe (4a)

Starts around the corner to the right of the previous climbs. Climb the thin crack to the overhang which is passed on the left to a ledge. Step left and climb over the bulges to the top.

33. Overhanging Wall 35ft. V.S. (4c)
Start just right of Via Anna. Climb the overhang direct.

34. Blind Alley 35ft. Diff.
The obvious chimney to the right of Overhanging Wall.

35. Broadway 35ft. V.S. (4c)
Climb the middle of the buttress to the right of the last climb. A boulder problem start.

To the right of Broadway the cliff is broken by a large grassy ramp; a useful descent.

36. Airlift 50ft. Severe
Start at the front of the buttress to the right of the grassy break. Climb up the face to a bulge and traverse round the arete to the left. Climb straight up, then move out on to the nose to finish. Exposed.

37. Fade Away 30ft. V.S. (4b)
Takes the arete throughout.

38. Sam Stretch 50ft. V.S. (4b)
Start up Airlift, but continue up and over the bulge to a ledge. Move up, and left, to pass the top bulge on rounded jugs.

39. Greasy Gully 25ft. Severe
The obvious gully to the right of Sam Stretch.

40. Left Wall 25ft. Severe
Climb the left wall of Greasy Gully to an awkward overhanging finish.

41. Greasy Wall 35ft. Hard V. Diff.
Climb the right wall of Greasy Gully using a flake.

42. Pencil Line 35ft. E3 (5b)
Start a few feet right of Greasy Gully below a faint peg scarred crack line. Ascend the overhang using fragile holds, and climb direct to the top. Bold.

43. Crocodile Chimney 35ft. Diff.
The chimney 20ft. right of Greasy Gully.

44. Monkey Puzzle 35ft. Diff.
Climb the wall to the right of the previous route on good holds. Move left and finish up the chimney.

45. Durius Melius 35ft. Hard V.S. (5b)
Follow Monkey Puzzle to the roof. Climb over the roof midway between Crocodile Chimney and Monkey Nut to a rounded ledge. Move right and surmount the top bulge at a pointed block.

46. Monkey Nut 35ft. V.S. (4b)
Follow Monkey Puzzle to the ledge. Move right and pass the bulge using a thin crack and rounded holds.

47. Telstar 40ft. V.S. (4c) *
Climb the corner right of Monkey Puzzle to a large block forming an overhang on the right. Climb over this and the bulging wall to a ledge. Climb this final overhang or escape right.

48. Montezumas Revenge 25ft. V.S. (5a)
Start 6ft. left of Roseberry Corner. Climb the slab to a bulging wall. Climb straight up this to the top, moving right at a prow.

49. Roseberry Corner 25ft. Hard Severe (4a)
The obvious corner 15 yds. right of Monkey Puzzle. The difficulties increase towards the top.

50. Ledges 20ft. V.S. (5a)
5ft. right of Roseberry Corner is an impending wall facing left. Climb the well defined ledges to a difficult finish.

TWIN BUTTRESS

Lies approximately 50 yds. right of Ledges, beyond Gun Buttress.

51. Castor 20ft. Diff.
Start at a spike at the foot of the left arm of the buttress and follow the ridge throughout.

52. Scout Crack 15ft. Diff.
The right hand of two cracks at the rear of the recess. Rather damp.

53. Pollux 25ft. Diff.
Climbs the right arm of the buttress, starting at a large embedded boulder. Climb the buttress direct with difficult moves at the start. A pleasant little climb.

BUTT END BUTTRESS

Lies approximately 30 yds. right of twin buttress.

54. Butt End Wall 20ft. Severe
Start to the left of the cleft formed by the detached buttress. Climb the wall split by horizontal cracks.

55. Smokey 25ft. Hard Diff.
Start in the cleft at its right end at the foot of a corner. Climb the corner and gain a shallow groove which is followed to the top.

To the right of Smokey is an alcove with a pinnacle forming its right wall.

56. Alcove Wall E1 (5c)
The left wall of the alcove.

57. Sooty 15ft. Severe
The climb takes the left hand rear corner.

58. Sweep 15ft. Hard V. Diff.
The right hand corner

59. Nutter 15ft. V.S. (4b)
Starts 20ft. right of Sweep in a hanging corner. Climb the corner finishing awkwardly.

THE WAINSTONES   G.R. 559036

These rocks, prominent on the skyline, are situated at the west end of Hasty Bank where the Cleveland Hills are dissected by Garfit Gap. The rocks themsleves are composed of sandstone with intrusions of iron. The crag has a traditional feel and can create a relaxed climbing atmosphere. A number of boulders provide interesting problems of all standards.

HISTORY

As far as can be ascertained, the first climber to explore the area was the late E.E. Roberts, who visited the Wainstones in 1906. Yet, in his modest way, Roberts wrote "odd visits don't count, some idle shepherd boy may have climbed here before me".

He was followed in 1912 by the brothers C.E. and D. Burrow and Canon Newton. They were joined by E. and G. Creighton, who were sufficiently keen to cycle from York - a round journey of more than 80 miles. In fact the visits of E. Creighton continued into the period of the First World War, when, armed with a revolver, he patrolled the rocks in the hours of darkness "looking for Zeppelins".

We then move on to 1928 when Arthur Barker and his brother, in the company of a select band of Teesside climbers known as the 'Bergers', and fired with enthusiasm by the climbing they had done in the Lake District, went looking for rocks nearer home. In the ensuing years Barker was instrumental in establishing most of the standard routes, among which were Bench Mark Crack, Ling Buttress, Sheep Walk Slab, The Bulge, and the ever popular Wall and Ledge. Concurrently with the 'Bergers', although climbing independently, several visits were paid by the brothers C.S. and T.H. Tilly in 1931 and 1932.

There followed a long period of inactivity until 1939 when J. Devenport and A. Parker came on the scene with Groove and Crack, Wall and Ledge Variations, and other routes.

HASTY BANK AREA 63

After the war A.P. Horne and M.F. Wilson straightened out many existing routes and finishes, although when a large fall of rock swept with it three of the older climbs, these were promptly replaced by Solomons Porch and Humpty Dumpty. A meet of the York M.C. in 1951 resulted in Tony Evenett leading the elusive Little Bo Peep.

Standards were now hardening, and C. Fielding's fine Sphinx Nose Traverse in 1954 was followed a year later by B. Mankin's ascent of the Steeple Face. T. Sullivan put up the attractive Central Route, following it in 1960 with Ali Baba, although a little aid was used on the latter. Five years later Tony Marr climbed the route without aid.

Recent years have yielded only a few new routes, notably Lemming Slab by Kelvin Neal and Chris Oswald (improved by Paul Ingham) and the equally hard Terrorist by Paul Ingham and Ian Dunn.

APPROACHES

Three approaches are described all enabling the crag to be reached comfortably in less than ½ hour.
1. Follow the approaches described for Ravenscar, but continue along the track until the rocks can be seen on the skyline.
2. From the summit of Clay Bank, ascend Hasty Bank to it's summit plateau and follow this west to the summit of the rocks.
3. ½ mile beyond Great Broughton on the Stokesley to Helmsley Road, follow the lane which continues to the foot of the hills. From the end of the lane a path leads steeply through the forest to the crags.

The rocks are situated on the 'nose' formed at the junction of the northwest facing Broughton Bank (Broughton Face) and the southwest facing side of Garfit Gap (Bilsdale Face).

The Wainstones Needle is prominent at the apex of these two faces.

BROUGHTON FACE - BROUGHTON BUTTRESS

The entire promontory of rock north of the main path.

1. Broughton Ridge   35ft.   Diff.
Starts at the extreme north-east (left) end of the buttress. Climb diagonally right on to a sloping foothold on the ridge of the buttress. Continue straight up to a ledge. Clamber up the face of a boulder and along its crest. Finish up the overhanging face of the summit block.

2. Bench-mark Crack   35ft.   Mild Severe
Lies immediately around the arete right of Broughton Ridge, and can be easily identified by a bench mark carved at its base. Ascend the crack and continue more easily to the top.

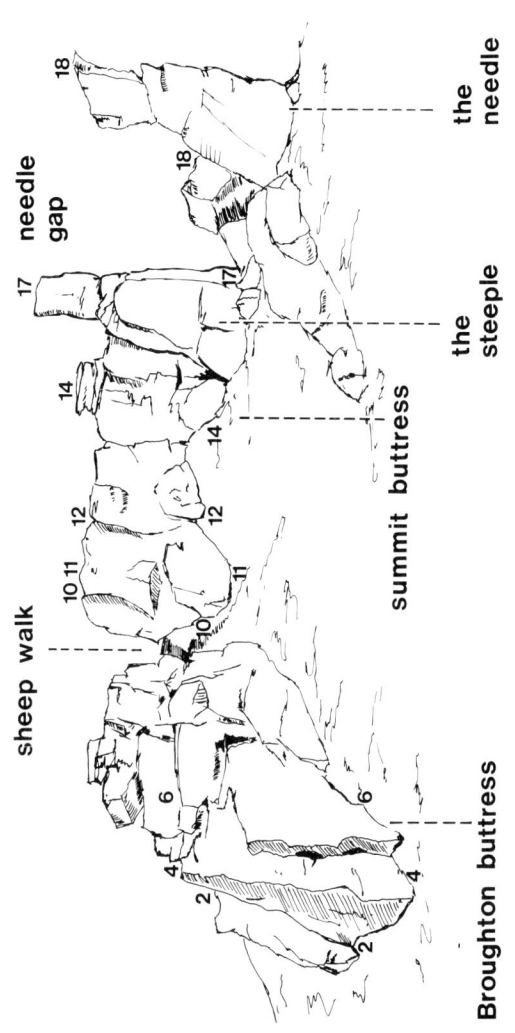

THE WAINSTONES – BROUGHTON FACE

HASTY BANK AREA

3. Psycho Syndicate　　25ft.　　E4 (6b)
The peg scarred wall to the right of Bench-Mark Crack is climbed free.

4. Tiny's Dilemma　　40ft.　　V.S. (4c)
Starts in a corner, just right of the lowest point of the rocks. Climb straight up the face just right of the arete. A good route.

5. Rookery Nook　　45ft.　　Diff.
Start at a chimney which bounds the right edge of the steep slab to the right of Tiny's Dilemma. The easy chimney is followed by a stomach traverse left for several feet, then finish up broken rocks above Tiny's Dilemma. A harder but more interesting start can be made by climbing the centre of the slab on small holds to gain the ledge.

6. Evening Wall　　25ft.　　Hard Diff.
Start just right of Rookery Nook on a sloping ledge. Climb the centre of the wall on small holds to a ledge, and then take the short corner on the right.

7. Milky Way　　35ft.　　Diff.
Start as for Rookery Nook. Climb the chimney until it finishes and continue up the face.

SHEEP WALK

The name given to that portion of the main path where it passes between Broughton Buttress and the main rocks. The next three climbs start from this path.

8. Sheep Walk Slab　　30ft.　　Mod.
Start to the right of the main path at the top of the slope. Traverse right on good holds for 10ft., then step up into a short chimney. Follow this to the top.

9. Green Wall　　25ft.　　V. Diff.
Start as for Sheep Walk Slab and continue straight up the vertical wall.

10. Flake, Wall and Crack　　20ft.　　Hard V. Diff.
Start at the flake embedded in the path. From the top of this, pull on to a large ledge. Finish up the twin cracks above.

11. Solomon's Porch　　35ft.　　Severe
Lies immediately around the corner to the right of the Flake. From a small block cross the wall to a vertical crack. Climb to a large ledge and ascend the overhanging buttress above.

12. Humpty Dumpty　　15ft.　　Diff.
Start 5ft. right behind large fallen blocks. Climb the obvious line up the face exposed by their fall.

13. Lurch　　15ft.　　Hard Severe (4a)
Climb the corner between Solomon's Porch and Humpty Dumpty. The name speaks for itself.

14. Novitiate   35ft.   Easy
Start just right of Lurch. Step up into a groove, and scramble to the right end of the summit blocks. Ascend the arete on large sloping footholds, moving left to finish.

BROUGHTON FACE - THE STEEPLE

The cleft tower which stands between the summit rocks and the Needle.

15. Steeple Goove   25ft.   Diff.
Start at the foot of a crack 10ft. right of Novitiate. Gain the crack over two large blocks and continue to the top of the Steeple.

16. Steeple Face   30ft.   Hard V.S. (5a)
Start at the lowest rocks left of Needle Gap (north side). Ascend the steep face with increasing difficulty to the top.

17. Steeple Chimney   30ft.   Diff.
Start at the same point as Steeple Face. Move right to the obvious wide crack and climb this to the top.

A depression, known as Needle Gap, now separates the Steeple from the Needle.

WAINSTONES NEEDLE

18. Main route   35ft.   Mod.
Start from the north side of Needle Gap. Ascend on good holds up a slab to the top block. Climb the left (southern) arete to the summit. Descent is by the same route.

19. North Route   25ft.   Hard V.S. (5a)
Start at the foot of the north corner of the Needle. Two easy steps are followed by hard moves over a bulge to the bracket above. A pull up lands one on the summit block.

20. The Girdle   35ft.   V. Diff.
The obvious crack 6ft. below the summit can be traversed.

BILSDALE FACE - THE STEEPLE AND SUMMIT BUTTRESS

21. Chop Yat Ridge   25ft.   V. Diff.
Start from the south east side of Needle Gap. Ascend the ridge of the Steeple for about 10ft. to a horizontal crack. Move right and continue up the wall on small holds.

22. Bird Lime   25ft.   E1 (5c)
Right of Chop Yat Ridge is a large embedded block. Fom this, step on to the wall and layback on small holds to an obvious jug. Continue in the same line to the top.

HASTY BANK AREA 67

23. Little Bo-Peep   35ft.   Hard Severe (4b)
Start around the corner right of Bird Lime. From the top of the first large block in the gully step left on to the face and hand traverse left for 8ft. Pull up on to a small ledge from where easier ground leads to the top.

24. Miss Muffet   30ft.   Hard Severe (4a)
Start as for Little Bo-Peep, but instead of the hand traverse climb straight up a small groove.

25. On Form   30ft.   Hard V.S. (5b)
Traverses Summit Buttress. Start as for Little Bo-Peep and follow the obvious horizontal break.

26. Cantilever   20ft.   Diff.
Scramble up the gully between Summit and Ling Buttresses to a point beneath the chockstone. Bridge up the Bilsdale side of the chimney to the chockstone, which is turned on the right.

BILSDALE FACE - LING BUTTRESS

This buttress lies to the right of the gully.

27. Peel Out   25ft.   E4 (6b)
Climb the overhanging wall immediately right of the gully. Continue up easier rocks to the top.

28. Ling Buttress   30ft.   Severe (4a)
On the front of the buttress to the right of Peel Out is a triangular depression. Climb to the apex of the triangle and make an awkward move left on to a slab, and continue to the top.

29. Groove and Crack   25ft.   V. Diff.
Start 5ft. right of the last climb. Follow easy rocks to gain a groove, and climb this diagonally left to a ledge. Climb the vertical crack above to finish.

30. Ling Corner   25ft.   Severe
Start as for Groove and Crack. Leave the bottom of the groove and climb a slab on the right. Finish directly up the vertical arete which bounds the right edge of the upper face of the buttress.

BILSDALE FACE - SPHINX ROCK

The prominent buttress right of Ling Buttress.

31. West Sphinx Climb   35ft.   Hard V.S. (5b)   **
Start just right of the lowest point of the rocks. Climb diagonally left to a small overhang and climb the left side of this with difficulty. Ascend direct to a prominent pocket then move right to a slab. Follow this to the summit. A very fine route.

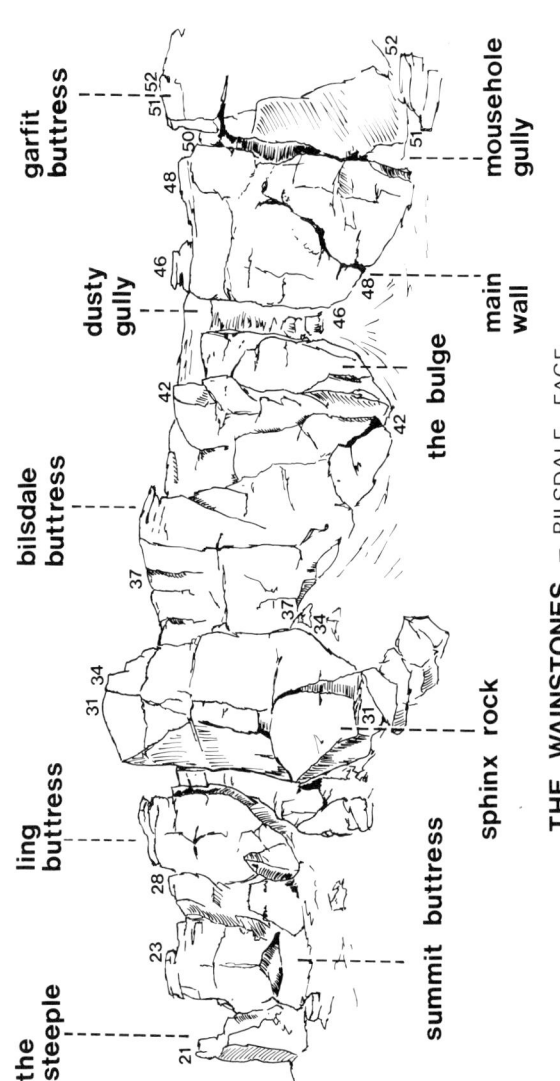

HASTY BANK AREA

31a. Direct Start   Hard V.S. (5c)
Left of the ordinary route is an obvious peapod. Climb past this to join the original route above the small overhang. This start is much harder for a short person.

32. Terrorist   30ft.   E4 (6a)
Start as for West Sphinx Climb. Climb to a small hanging groove (peg runner, not in situ) move slightly right and climb up to join Sphinx Nose Traverse. Continue direct to the top. A serious route.

33. East Sphinx Climb   30ft.   Hard V.S. (5a)
Start 5ft. right of Terrorist, below a short crack. Climb the wall, using some layback holds, and finish up the crack.

34. Sphinx Nose Traverse   35ft.   Severe   **
Start 5ft. right of East Sphinx Climb, in a sandy gully. Climb diagonally left to a short crack, then traverse delicately left, following an obvious break, to the arete. Left of the arete is a slab, which is climbed on flutes to the top. An enjoyable classic.

35. Traverse of the Gods   30ft.   E1 (5b)
A horizontal crack cuts across both faces of Sphinx Rock. The route traverses this crack from left to right passing under a small nose and then under Sphinx Nose Traverse.

Immediately right of the upper end of the sandy gully flanking Sphinx Rock is a trinity of parallel cracks, spaced about 5ft. apart.

36. Pip   15ft.   Diff.

37. Squeak   15ft.   Diff.

38. Wilfred   15ft.   Diff.

BILSDALE BUTTRESS

The buttress lying to the right of Sphinx Rock.

39. Jackdaw Ridge   20ft.   V. Diff.
Climbs the ridge on the left side of Bilsdale Buttress. Climb the ridge for a few feet until a short traverse leads left across the face. Finish straight up.

40. Jackdaw Wall   25ft.   Hard V.S. (5c)
Start just left of Jackdaw Ridge. A layback move leads to small holds. Follow these until a long reach enables the top to be gained. An artificial but bold route.

41. Jackdaw Gully 30ft. Mod.
The obvious narrow gully right of Jackdaw Ridge.

42. Christopher 30ft. Hard Severe (4b)
Ascend Jackdaw Gully to a ledge then traverse right across the wall until an awkward move enables a slabby groove to be reached.

43. Bulge Superdirect 25ft. Hard V.S. (5c)
Start at the foot of a slim groove 5ft. right of Jackdaw Gully. Climb the face just right of the groove on small awkward holds. The groove can be climbed direct (6a).

44. The Bulge 35ft. Severe (4a)
Start from the foot of Dusty Gully. Move up for a few feet, then work left across the face to finish up the slab right of Christopher.

45. Bulge Direct 30ft. Severe (4a)
Start as for the Bulge. Climb straight up to a slab, and continue bearing slightly left to the top.

Dusty Gully *seperates Bilsdale Buttress from Main Wall and offers a quick unpleasant descent.*

BILSDALE FACE - MAIN WALL

46. The Slab Climb 30ft. V. Diff.
Start at the left of the face and ascend the slab to a ledge. Finish directly above.

47. Central Route 30ft. V.S. (4c)
Climb the centre of the face via an obvious awkward mantleshelf at half height.

48. Wall and Ledge 35ft. Diff. *
Start below a prominent crack on the right of the face. Climb the crack to a large ledge and then follow a small corner to the top.

48a. Variation 20ft. V. Diff.
Start around the corner to the right of the normal route, below an obvious mantleshelf. Climb this and continue up the wall to the large ledge of the ordinary route.

49. Concave Wall 25ft. Hard V.S. (5b)
Start as for Wall and Ledge Variation, then climb up rightwards until an awkward move leads to good holds. Continue direct to the top.

50. Mousehole Gully 30ft. Mod.
The obvious chimneys right of Concave Wall.

HASTY BANK AREA

GARFIT BUTTRESS

The impressive buttress which bounds the extreme right end of Bilsdale face.

51. **Lemming Slab**   30ft.   E3 (5c)
Start in the centre of the front face of the buttress. Climb straight up to the second of two small ledges, then traverse left to the arete. Make some blind moves to gain better holds and follow these to the top.

52. **Ali Baba**   30ft.   E1 (5b)   **
Start below the prominent groove right of Lemming Slab. Climb the groove until a move left can be made through the overhangs to a wide horizontal crack. Ascend direct to the top. A superb route.

53. **Sesame**   30ft.   E1 (5b)
Follow Ali Baba until a traverse right can be made around a corner to a wide crack. Finish up this.

54. **Garfit Face**   20ft.   Hard V.S. (5a)
Start at the extreme right end of Garfit Buttress. Climb the arete until it is possible to move left to the wide crack of Sesame.

55. **Turkish Delight**   45ft.   E2 (5c)
The obvious traverse line of Garfit Buttress. Start as for Garfit Face and finish as for Lemming Slab.

56. **Lofty's Ease**   20ft.   Diff.
Start at the same point as Garfit Face. Traverse right to the rear of the buttress and then climb the arete. A long reach helps.

LOWER WAINSTONES

Some distance below the Needle lies a jumble of boulders. These well scratched rocks provide interesting boulder problems of all standards.

COLD MOOR   G.R. 553034

From the Needle a jumble of boulders can be seen on the east side of Cold Moor across Garfit Gap. These give some fine boulder problems and a few very short routes.

GARFIT QUARRY

This quarry lies on the south east edge of Hasty Bank, and can be seen from the right side of the Wainstones. It is very small, reaching a maximum height of 20ft., and is again a good place to spend a few hours bouldering. The central crackline gives a particularly good problem (5c).

72 SCUGDALE AREA

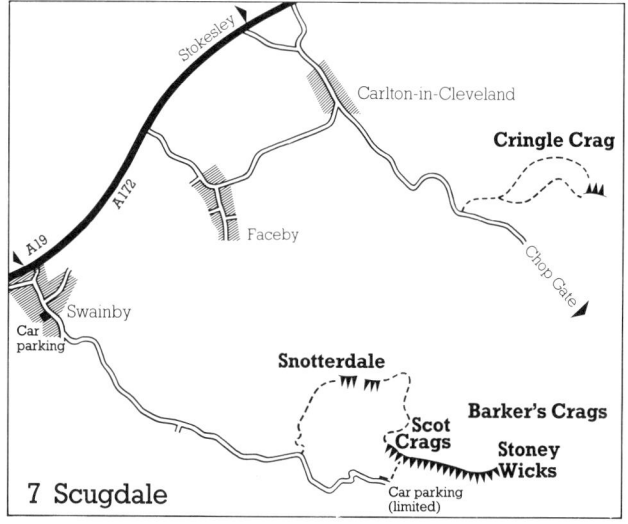

Scugdale Area

SCOT CRAGS AND BARKER'S CRAGS   G.R. 520004

The crags lie at 1,000 ft. above sea level, on the north side of the Scugdale valley along the edge of the open moorland between the subsidiary valley of Snotterdale and the neck of land crossed by the old pony track from Scugdale Hall to the Carlton/Chop Gate road.

The rocks, which are of middle Jurassic sandstone, are mostly in the form of large blocks rather than a continuous edge. Though never more than 30 ft. high they yield over 120 climbs of considerable variety and charm, with many high quality problems which, due to their short length, have not been starred. They face 15° west of south, are quick to dry even in winter, and are often sheltered in windy conditions.

In the following description it has been convenient to divide the rocks into a number of 'buttresses'; this term is applied rather loosely and the diagrams should be sought for exact location of the climbs.

Due to the short nature of the climbs it has been decided to drop the adjectival grade on routes harder than severe in standard. On these routes only the technical grade will be given.

HISTORY

The bouldering nature of the climbing did not inspire the early pioneers to record their achievements. However, starting in 1939, A.W. Evans produced a large number of climbs and developed an intimate knowledge of the rocks. By the late '50s the rocks were substantially developed. However, the significant rise in standards starting in the late '70s produced further high quality routes, notably Alan Taylor's New Dimensions.

APPROACHES

The normal approach is from Swainby (which lies just off the A 172), by following the narrow road up the Scugdale valley. There are a few parking places just before the Nursery at the end of the road. In order not to prejudice future access to this popular climbing ground please observe the following points:

1. Drive carefully along the Scugdale valley. There have been many accidents involving climbers.
2. Park sensibly off the road and do not block any access to fields. Remember to allow room for the extra width of farm machinery.
3. No dogs allowed.
4. Do not park in the Nursery Car Park.

SCOT CRAGS

These are the left-hand group of rocks.

NO. 1 BUTTRESS - RAKE'S BUTTRESS

The buttress at the extreme left (west) end of the crag.

1. Uncle's 20ft. 4c
The wall is ascended using three obvious small pockets.

2. Straight and Narrow 20ft. Mod.
Start just left of the toe of the buttress. Move up and right to the base of a grooved wall, ascend this to the top.

3. Easy Stages 20ft. Mod.
Climb the overhang on its right side.

ORIEL WALL

About 12 yds. to the right of Rake's Buttress.

4. Mounting Block 10ft. Diff.
The wall below and just right of the conspicuous protruding block is climbed.

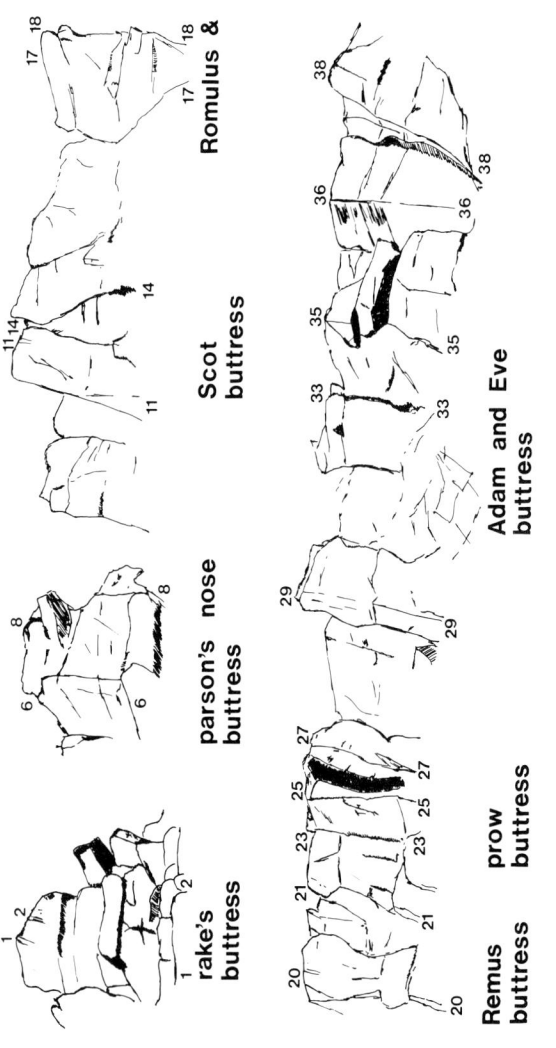

5. The Nutcrackers   10ft.   Diff.
The short crack with an undercut base 7 yds. right of 4.

NO. 2 BUTTRESS - THE PARSON'S NOSE

6. Jivers Wall   15ft.   4c
Goes up the centre of the left-hand wall on small holds. Harder if you are short.

7. Bop Route   15ft.   V. Diff.
The steep corner right of Jivers Wall.

8. Zoot Route   10ft.   Hard Diff.
Climbs the steep wall finishing just left of the Parson's Nose.

NO. 3 BUTTRESS - SCOT BUTTRESS

The slabs at the left-hand end of the buttress provide two easy routes.

9. Hadrian's Wall   15ft.   Severe
Climbs straight up the middle of the left-hand wall on small holds.

10. Corner Direct   20ft.   Severe
The left-hand corner is climbed direct.

11. Nook and Cranny   20ft.   V. Diff.
Climb the corner direct to the nook, traverse right and ascend direct to the top.

12. Highland Fling   20ft.   5a
Move straight up the rounded corner to the left of Bawbee Crack on sketchy holds.

13. Bawbee Crack   20ft.   Diff.
Mount the block at the foot of the crack and then straight up. Doubtful jammed stone.

14. Blaeberry Crack   20ft.   Diff.
The crack to the right of Bawbee Crack, joining it at the top.

15. Blaeberry Buttress   15ft.   Mod.
Start right of the arete, move round to the left and up on good footholds to the top.

NO.4 BUTTRESS - ROMULUS AND REMUS

16. Wolf Wall   15ft.   V. Diff.
The left-hand end of the west wall.

17. Woodpecker Wall   20ft.   V. Diff.
Goes up the right-hand end of the west wall using well defined pocket holds on the upper slab.

18. Romulus   20ft.   V. Diff.
The front of the buttress is climbed.

19. Tiber Chimney   20ft.   Easy
The easy chimney between Romulus and Remus.

20. Remus   25ft.   4c
Broken by a large shelf but a pleasant pitch. The top has two alternatives, either straight up the centre or the right-hand arete.

NO. 5 BUTTRESS - THE PROW

21. Halyards   20ft.   V. Diff.
Straight up the left-hand arete.

22. Little-by-Little   15ft.   V. Diff.
The wall to the right of Halyards.

23. Main Mast Crack   15ft.   Severe
The well-defined corner crack. Strenuous.

24. Stewker   20ft.   5b
The wall right of Main Mast Crack. The landing can be nasty.

25. The Prow   20ft.   5a
The obvious prow right of Stewker. Crux is near the top.

26. Galley Chimney   15ft.   Easy
The chimney right of the Prow.

27. The Bulkhead   15ft.   4b
The wall right of the chimney by an ill-defined crack.

NO. 6 BUTTRESS - ADAM & EVE

Eve is the prominent pillar of rock to the right of the prow. Adam is the small outcrop behind and slightly to the left.

28. Jill's Delight   10ft.   Mod.
Goes up the left hand arete of Adam.

29. Jack's Delight   20ft.   4c
Start at bottom corner of Eve and move across left and up centre of the left wall.

30. Eve   20ft.   5a/5b
The arete can be climbed on either side. The left side is 5a, the right side 5b.

SCUGDALE AREA

31. Serpent   20ft.   5c
The right wall of Eve has a prominent crackline going rightwards. Move up to this and follow it till small pockets lead left and to the top. A very serious lead.

Immediately below Serpent is a jumble of boulders which form a cave which can be used by up to eight people in bad weather.

32. Green Wall   10ft.   Mod.
Behind and to the right of the cave in a bay.

33. Archer's Crack   10ft.   V. Diff.
The lower part is climbed as a layback until holds can be used on the slab on the right.

34. Clarance   12ft.   5b
The wall right of Archer's Crack.

35. The Pulpit   15ft.   5b
The obvious nose of rock. Climb the crack on the left-hand side till a traverse line right can be reached. Traverse right to the arete. Move up (crux) to the top. A very serious pitch. Can be led.

35a. Direct start   5b
The climb can be started direct.

36. The Choir   15ft.   Severe
This block of rock provides one pitch which starts slightly to the right of the overhanging front and then goes straight up the wall.

NO. 7 BUTTRESS - DRUNKEN BUTTRESS

A tilted block forming a slab on its left side and two overhanging faces.

37. Seamy Side   20ft.   Mod.
Start at the left edge and climb this all the way.

38. Hangover   20ft.   4c
The right-hand edge of the slab has an overhung groove at its base. The main difficulty lies in gaining the slab.

39. Tippling Wall   20ft.   5a
To the right of Hangover is an overhanging wall. Ascend this on small holds.

40. The Shelf   15ft.   5b
Climb the wall to the right of Tippling Wall which has an obvious green shelf at two-thirds height.

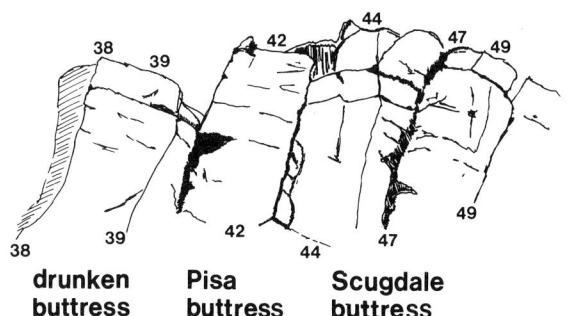

drunken buttress   **Pisa buttress**   **Scugdale buttress**

NO. 8 BUTTRESS - PISA

This is the leaning rock to the right of Drunken Buttress.

41. Plumb Line 12ft. Severe
The slanting crack between Drunken Buttress and Pisa. Awkward.

42. Gravity Wall 20ft. 4b
Start on the right, move diagonally left, then straight up to the top.

43. Galileo's Gully 20ft. Severe
An exercise in bridging. Climb the outside of the chimney. If finished inside it reduces the standard to moderate.

NO. 9 BUTTRESS - SCUGDALE BUTTRESS

44. Tooth and Nail 25ft. Severe
Good but widely spaced holds enable the lower part of the wall to be climbed, after which move left and up to the top.

45. Hybrid 25ft. Severe
Start up Scugdale Chimney, move round the corner to the left and then traverse upwards to the same finish as Tooth and Nail.

46. Supine 25ft. 4b
A start is made on the arete taking a line to the right of Hybrid. Finish over the overhangs.

47. Scugdale Chimney 25ft. Diff.
The prominent curving chimney.

48. Scugdale Chimney Eliminate 25ft. 4c
Climb the chimney to where it moves right, then move straight over the overhang to the top.

49. Zeta Wall 20ft. Severe
The wall right of Scugdale Chimney up the obvious zig-zag crack. A fine pitch.

50. Deviator 20ft. 5a
Start right of Zeta Wall below a shallow groove. Climb the groove direct to an awkward finish.

51. Nameless Crack 15ft. V. Diff.
The obvious crack right of Deviator.

NO. 10 BUTTRESS - BARKER'S BUTTRESS

52. Cub's Climb 20ft. Diff.
Goes up the left end of the south-west wall. Its bark is worse than its bite.

53. Pup's Climb 20ft. V. Diff.
Goes up 6ft. right of Cub's Climb. Rather harder.

54. Bonzo 20ft. 5b
Climbs the wall 6ft. right of Pup's Climb. Hard move in mid-height.

55. Pets' Corner 20ft. 4c
The prominent arete is climbed on its S.W. side.

56. Whippet Wall 20ft. 4c
Straight up the south-east wall.

57. Barker's Chimney 15ft. Mod.
The obvious chimney.

58. Cat-Walk 20ft. Diff.
The wall right of Barker's Chimney. Start on right and move up and across to finish at top of previous route.

59. Pluto 20ft. 4c
Ascends the right-hand edge of the wall.

60. Cerberus Crack 10ft. Severe
The crack to the right of Pluto.

80 SCUGDALE AREA

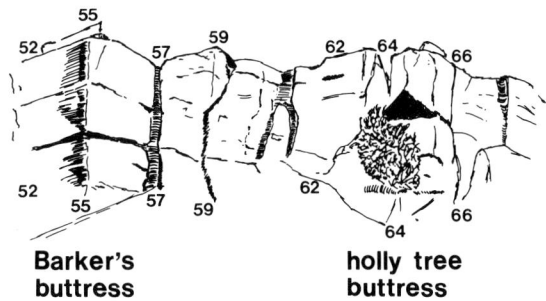

Barker's buttress **holly tree buttress**

61. Peke's Perch   10ft.   V. Diff.
The wall right of Cerberus Crack has a well-defined small niche. Ascend the wall via this.

NO. 11 BUTTRESS - HOLLY TREE BUTTRESS

62. Pingers   20ft.   5a
Climbs the centre of the wall to the left of the holly. Variations can be made on left and right.

63. Prickly Rib   20ft.   Diff.
Start up the right-hand edge of the slab forming the left wall of Holly Tree Chimney and continue up the rib to the top.

64. Holly-Tree Chimney   25ft.   Diff.
To the right of the holly is a slab under a prominent overhang. The slab is crossed from right to left to the chimney. Ascend this to the top.

65. Holly Tree Hover   20ft.   4c
Start right of the Holly Tree Chimney, climb the wall and cracks right of the overhang. A direct can be made straight over the overhang. The landing is obvious (Prickly).

66. Saint's Wall   20ft.   V. Diff.
The obvious crack and niche to the right of the last climb.

67. The Mantleshelf   20ft.   V. Diff.
The obvious bulging slab right of Saint's Wall. Climb the slab to the overhang, mantleshelf over this. Awkward.

68. Humpty Dumpty   20ft.   4b
The bulging wall right of the Mantleshelf. Do not use the chimney on right.

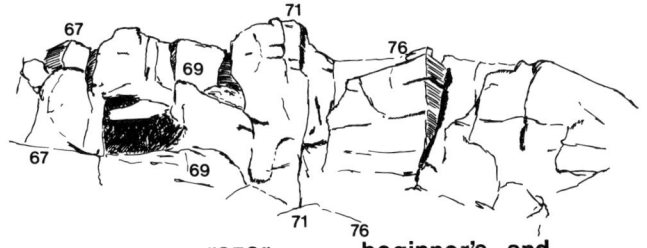

SCOT CRAGS razor buttress beginner's and curtain slabs

NO. 12 BUTTRESS - THE RAZOR

69. Slashed Wall 10ft. Diff.
The short grooved wall with awkward holds.

70. The Gash 10ft. Diff.
A tricky corner.

71. Razor Rib 25ft. V. Diff.
The rib is climbed slightly to the left of the edge. The right side of the rib can be climbed, the grade being 5a.

72. The Strop 15ft. Mod.
To the right of Razor Rib is a wall with a curving ledge which is followed to Razor Rib above the difficult start.

73. Suds 15ft. 5a
Climb the thin crack above The Strop.

74. Tension 15ft. 5b.
The steep wall right of Suds.

NO. 13 BUTTRESS - Two Slabs

(a) Beginner's Slab

75. Alpha 20ft. Easy
The easy groove on the left.

76. Beta 20ft. Mod.
The well-scratched route up the centre.

77. Gamma 15ft. Diff.
The right-hand edge.

(b) Curtain Slab 15ft. Diff.
There are a number of short pitches on the deeply grooved slab to the right of (a).

GIRDLE TRAVERSES

It has been left to the individual to discover traverses and problems of a climbing wall nature. However the traverse from the right hand end of Barker's Buttress to the left end of Drunken Buttress is worth noting and is grade 5a (maybe 5b across Drunken Buttress).

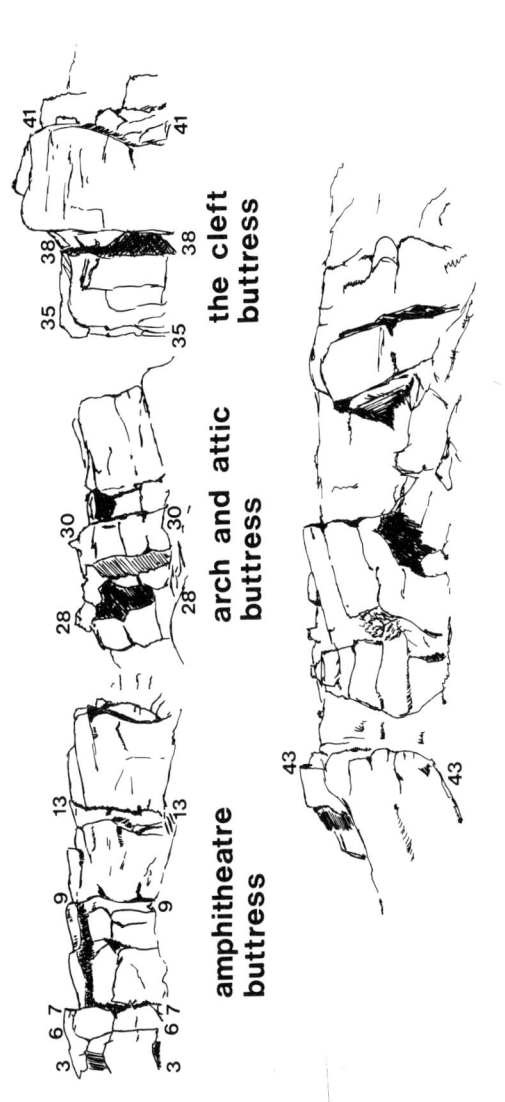

BARKER'S CRAGS

These lie to the right of the drystone wall at the east end of Scot Crags. There are many boulder problems in the 200 yards between the drystone wall and No. 14 Buttress on the right.

NO. 14 BUTTRESS - AMPHITHEATRE BUTTRESS

1. Green Chimney   10ft.   V. Diff.
To the left of the corner is a prominent chimney with an overhanging finish.

2. Outer Wall   15ft.   Severe
Starts a couple of feet left of Pedestal Crack, finishing just left of it. Strenuous

3. Pedestal Crack   15ft.   Severe
The narrow crack to the left of the Nose.

4. The Nose   15ft.   Mod.
Starts slightly to the right of the Nose and then moves up the edge.

5. Pedestal Chimney   10ft.   Mod.
The first crack to the right of the nose.

6. Pedestal Wall   20ft.   V. Diff.
Start up Pedestal Chimney, move right on to the face and climb this to the top.

7. Flake Chimney   15ft.   Diff.
A thin, vertical flake runs up the middle of the chimney, which lies in the left-hand corner of the Amphitheatre.

8. Flake Chimney Wall   15ft.   Mod.
Starts up (7) then moves to the right across the slab and finishes up the first crack.

9. Long Chimney   15ft.   Diff.
Lies in the corner left of a prominent nose.

10. Easter Edge   15ft.   5c
The arete right of Long Chimney.

11. Fairy Tale High   15ft.   6a
The wall right of Long Chimney.

12. The Nose   15ft.   5c
The prominent nose right of Long Chimney.

13. Alcove Chimney   20ft.   Severe
In the right-hand corner of the Amphitheatre is a deep cut vertical crack bounded by a smooth wall. This is Alcove Chimney.

14. Alcove Cracks   20ft.   Severe
Left of Alcove Chimney is a steep groove enclosed by two narrow cracks, this is Alcove Cracks.

15. Alan's Wall   20ft.   5a
The wall right of Alcove Chimney.

16. Snatch Arete   20ft.   5c
The arete right of Alcove Chimney.

17. Pioneer's Chimney   15ft.   Mod.
The chimney right of Alcove Cracks.

18. Ancient's Ascent   15ft.   Diff.
Lies on the right-hand side of the flake forming the right wall of Pioneer's Chimney and keeps to the left edge.

80 yards to the right:

NO. 15 BUTTRESS - ROAD END BUTTRESS

A thick slab forms the left wall of a chimney and the left (outer) side of this provides:

19. One for the Road   15ft.   Diff.
The edge of the slab in the form of a nose.

20. Shandy   20ft.   Mod.
A pleasant pitch.

21. Chaser Chimney   15ft.   Diff.
The obvious chimney.

30 yards to the right:

22. Last But One Buttress   15ft.   V. Diff.
It provides a 10ft. layback followed by a corner.

30 yards to the right:

NO. 16 BUTTRESS - DAY'S END BUTTRESS

23. Flake Wall   10ft.   Severe
The steep wall on the left.

24. Joshua's Nose   15ft.   Diff.
The nose formed by the right-hand end of Flake Wall.

25. **Bilberry Cracks** 15ft. Severe
Round to the right is a groove edged by two narrow cracks.

26. **Belly Chimney** 15ft. Diff.
Further to the right is a wide chimney containing two cracks.

27. **Jericho Wall** 10ft. Diff.
The wall right of Belly Chimney.

160 yards right across an old sunken track:

NO. 17 BUTTRESS - ARCH AND ATTIC

28. **Arch Gully** 20ft. Mod.
A pleasant all weather climb.

29. **Fallen Arch** 15ft. 5a
To the right of the arch is a thin overhanging jam crack which is difficult to start and leave.

29a. **Foot Loose** 15ft. 5c
Start about 15ft. right of Fallen Arch. Start in the middle of a leaning wall. Pull up and move left to finish up a short thin finger crack and sloping ledge.

30. **Attic Gully** 15ft. Mod.
To the right of Fallen Arch.

31. **Hogmanay** 10ft. V. Diff.
30 yards to the right is a large block split by a horizontal crack and a vertical crack above. The route takes this.

32. **First Footing** 10ft. Mod.
The corner right of Hogmanay.

33. **Black Corner** 10ft. V. Diff.
Is the left arete of the next piece of rock. Climb straight up.

20 yards further right:

NO. 18 BUTTRESS - THE CLEFT BUTTRESS

The highest part of the series

34. **Leaning Wall** 20ft. 4c
Goes up the left corner of the buttress, moving slightly to the left.

35. **The Chute** 20ft. 4c
Start as for (34) but moves up and over the scoop slightly to the right.

SCUGDALE AREA

36. Finger Jam 20ft. 5c
Start below the obvious thin crack, ascend this moving left at the top and pull up to finish as for the Chute.

37. New Dimensions 20ft. 5c
Start to the right of Finger Jam below a wide crack. Ascend the wall direct using lots of awkward and contrived manoeuvres. A very good sustained climb. The landing is fortunately excellent.

38. Chockstone Chimney 20ft. Diff.
The obvious chimney.

39. Sculptured Wall 25ft. 5a
The right wall of Chockstone Chimney.

40. Sculptured Arete 25ft. 5c
Ascend Sculptured Wall for a couple of feet, then climb the right arete till a traverse right can be made followed by awkward moves to the top. A serious climb.

41. Night Entry 30ft. Severe
Climbs the overhanging crack 20′ right of (40) followed by the buttress above.

42. Rum Doodle 30ft. 4b
To the right of Night Entry is a prominent layback which is climbed. Finish as for Night Entry.

100 yards further right:

NO. 19 BUTTRESS - CINDERELLA

Is sub-divided into three buttresses.

43. Cinderella 20ft. Mod.
This is the left-hand and highest buttress, climb the nose.

44. The Ugly Sisters 15ft. V. Diff.
The other two smaller buttresses can both be climbed at this standard on their left sides.

55 yards right lies:

NO. 20 BUTTRESS - THE VIRGIN

45. The Virgin 20ft. 4c
Climb up the left wall.

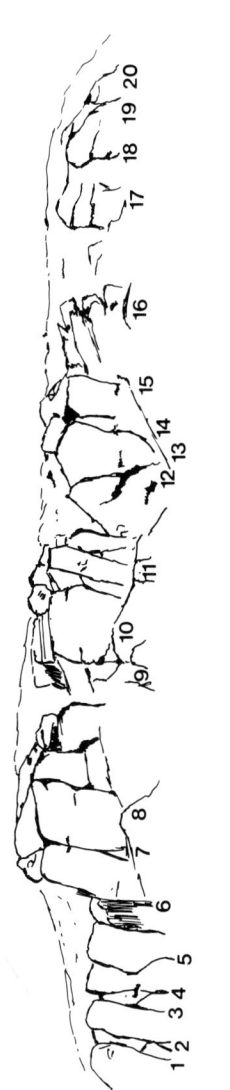

STONEY WICKS

46. Right Wall Route 15ft. Severe
Climb the right wall of the buttress.

STONEY WICKS

This small outcrop is at the extreme right-hand (east) of the series, 125 yards from the Virgin Buttress. The height is small, up to 15ft., but this compact stretch of rock gives numerous boulder problems on a harder and rougher rock than the rest of Scugdale. The following are the names and standards of some of the climbs which may be located by reference to the sketch.

1. Introductory	Mod.	
2. Layback Slab	Severe	
3. Crackers	V. Diff.	
4. Loopy	V. Diff.	
5. Loony	V. Diff.	
6. Toper's Trouble	V. Diff.	
7. Y-Crack	V. Diff.	
8. Sobersides	Hard V. Diff.	
9. Free and Easy	Mod.	
10. Nondescript	V. Diff.	
11. Lambda	Diff.	
12. Tombstone	Diff.	
13. Sepulchre	Hard V. Diff.	
14. Hanging Chimney	V. Diff.	
15. Waltzing Matilda	Mod.	
16. Solitary	Diff.	
17. Corner Climb	V. Diff.	
18. Twisting Crack	Mod.	
19. Flake Slab	Diff.	
20. Pocket Wall	Diff.	

SNOTTERDALE   G.R. 513013

So called because 'it's not a dale'. The crags lie in trees and are not easy to find.

APPROACHES

Go up Scugdale, as for Scot Crags, but leave the road at Sparrow Hall. Pass behind Fog Close to the rim of the moor when a path is followed to the top of the crags. Allow 25 minutes.

CASTLE BUTTRESS

Spider's Eliminate　　30ft.　　Hard V.S. (4c)
The well defined crack on the left hand side of the buttress. Climb the overhang and crack above by either bold laybacking or very awkward jamming. A good route.

Spider's Web　　30ft.　　Hard V.S. (5a)
Start at Spider's Eliminate, move out left to a small ledge, then up passing another ledge to gain a short corner and thus the top.

Desperandum　　30ft.　　E2 (5c)
A series of cracks left of No. 2 route are climbed with great difficulty but excellent protection. A superb route.

No. 2 Route　　35ft.　　Mild Severe
A prominent chimney divides the buttress into two parts. Climb the cracks just left of the chimney. Finish up the bulging slab on the left.

C.R. Crack　　35ft.　　V. Diff.
The chimney is climbed to a ledge. Finish up the right-hand crack.

Slings　　30ft.　　Hard V.S. (5b)
The arete, 15ft. to the right of C.R. Crack, is climbed on the right-hand side. Move round the arete and up to the top. Poorly protected.

Fissure　　30ft.　　Diff.
Start as for Slings, move right up the diagonally sloping crack to the holly. Finish up the crack on the left.

SNOTTERDALE RIGHT HAND　　　　　　　　G.R. 513014

HISTORY

The crag was discovered by members of the C.M.C., but nothing was recorded. It was redeveloped by S. Brown, D. Paul and friends.

APPROACHES

Same approach as for the Snotterdale Crag. Once above these rocks walk ¼ mile due east and descend through some trees over the remnants of a wall to the East end of the crag.

SCUGDALE AREA

UPPER TIER

The routes are described from right to left.

OWL BUTTRESS

The small wedge shaped buttress at the right end.

David & Goliath   15ft.   Hard Severe (4a)
The wall on well brushed slots.

Myth   15ft.   Mild V.S. (4b)
The crack to the right of Soothsayer.

Soothsayer   20ft.   E1 (5b)
The wall on the left of the buttress is climbed direct.

MAIN WALL

Keep Crack   15ft.   Severe
20 yds. left of Soothsayer. Climb the crack starting off a grassy ledge at mid-height.

Sixth Sense   20ft.   E3 (6a)
The wall on the left of Keep Crack climbed via three small pockets.

Saxon   20ft.   E1 (5b)
The crack in the middle of the wall with a large tree growing out of the top.

Somnium   35ft.   E3 (6a)
The faint groove line above the overhang is gained via a series of undercuts over the roof then up the groove. Finish the wall direct.

V. Groove Climb   20ft.   V. Diff.
The obvious groove 50 yds. left of Saxon. Climb the groove left of the square roof. Scramble to finish.

LOWER TIER

The Wall   20ft.   E1 (5c)
The wall to the right of the arete.

Excalibur   25ft.   Mild V.S. (4b)
The impressive arete to the left of the Wall.

Brick 20ft. V.S. (4c)
The Wall and groove 10ft. right of the Wall.

Mid Height 15ft. V.S. (5a)
The crack on the end of the buttress is climbed direct.

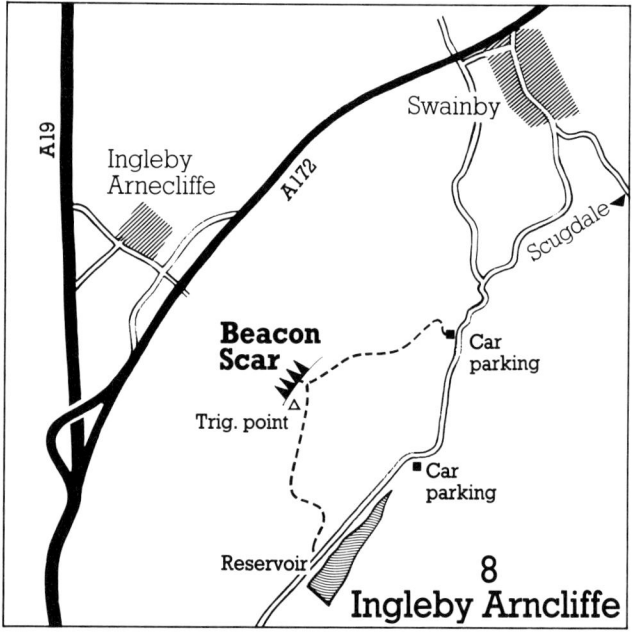

Ingleby Arncliffe Area

BEACON SCAR   G.R. 460998

The crag is fairly good quality sandstone, but some climbs exit on to steep shale which can require special care. The area around the crag is heavily wooded and because of this the rock can remain green for some time after rain, especially in winter. However, the crag is well worth visiting as some of the climbs rank with the best in the area.

HISTORY

The first to appreciate the potential of Beacon Scar were J. Clark and N.A. Thompson, the latter adding Sunnyside and Alligator Crawl and other routes on Scarth Wood Buttress. J. Hickman and M. Wilson modestly added their quota.

T. Sullivan made an ascent of the elusive Beacon Buttress and in 1960 added the superb line of Gehenna, still one of the finest routes in the area. In 1965 M. Railton visited Beacon Scar and climbed the much attempted corner to the right of the Boss, naming it Nail File.

During the 1970's M. Readshaw added the Flying Trapeze, a high level girdle of the Boss, and free ascents were made of both Tremor & Mongol. In 1979 P. Ingham climbed Yellow Peril and then with T. Marr, Skateboard. Finally K. Neal led the hard Epicentre.

APPROACHES

Beacon Scar is situated about a mile to the south-east of Ingleby Arncliffe. It is possible to walk up the hillside above Arncliffe Hall but a better approach is to leave the road between Swainby and Osmotherly about 200 yards after the cattle grid at the top of Shepherd's Hill. A small car park is available. From the car park follow a broad track, which leads off to the right, and then across the moor westwards for ¾ mile (Lyke Wake Walk). Pass through a gate and then a second gate on the right into the plantation. Now bear right through the trees for about 100 yards, to the top of Scarth Wood Buttress. Walking time for both routes is about 20 minutes.

The crag is divided into West and North Faces, to the left and right respectively of the central watercourse. Descents can be found at either end of the crag or just north of the central watercourse.

WEST FACE

The whole of the crag to the left of the central watercourse. At the left end of the West Face is an isolated buttress.

SCARTH WOOD BUTTRESS

Penguin Crack   25ft.   Diff.
Start in the corner of the gully opposite the ivy wall. Climb straight up on good holds.

Sunnyside   50ft.   Diff.
Start 30ft. right of Penguin Crack at a chockstone forming twin cracks. Climb up the slab on the left to a tree in the gully, then traverse left to a tree on the corner and finish straight up.

Sunnyside Direct   25ft.   V.S. (4b)
Start to the left of the ordinary route and climb the corner groove to gain the slab of the normal route. Very pleasant.

Tree Gully   35ft.   Mod.
Start as for Sunnyside. Climb the gully to the tree. Finish by climbing up a crack in the short wall and then up left to the summit.

Honeysuckle Chimney   45ft.   Mod.
The chimney and slabs 8ft. from Tree Gully are climbed.

Alligator Crawl   50ft.   V. Diff.
Start from a large boulder 50ft. to the right of Scarth Wood Buttress. A short cleft is followed by an awkward move on to a ledge. Traverse left along the ledge and up a narrow slab to the final chimney.

Direct Start   15ft.   V.S. (4b)
Start 15ft. left of the ordinary start in a corner. Climb the corner crack to finish up the final chimney. An introduction to the harder cracks.

After Hours   35ft.   Hard Severe (4b)
Start 10ft. right of the direct start to Alligator Crawl and climb the crack system, to cross Alligator Crawl. Continue Direct to the top.

Yellow Peril   35ft.   E2 (5c)
Climbs a slanting groove and crack on the wall left of Mongol. Climb the groove with a difficult move to get establishment on a round ledge, sapling runner. Continue up a crack.

Mongol   70ft.   E2 (5c)   **
Start about 30ft. right of the Direct Start to Alligator Crawl from a ledge below the thin Y crack splitting the wall. Climb the crack (strenuous) until a hard move can be made to gain a ledge high on the right. Climb a deceptive little groove above. A superb climb. A variation finish can be made on the left of the one described.

The wall to the right of Mongol has been climbed at Hard V.S. (5b), but is not recommended for obvious reasons.

ARNCLIFFE SLAB

The large slab flanking the left of the Boss.

Sunset   60ft.   V. Diff.
Start close to the left edge of the slab. Climb straight up to better holds on the edge and then climb the wall above by a groove on the left.

Evensong   60ft.   Diff.
Start from a rock embedded in the roots of a tree. Climb the short chimney beneath an oak and then the groove. Finish directly up the wall.

Vespers   50ft.   Diff.
The crack 6ft. right of Evensong is climbed finishing either side of the protruding block.

Matins   50ft.   Diff.
Climb the corner to the left of The Boss.

The Boss   70ft.   A2
Start below the prominent big overhang. Free climb to the roof (Hard V.S.), climb this on bolts. From a ledge over the lip free climb to the top (Hard Severe). A fun route?

The Flying Trapeze   150ft.   V.S. (4b, 4c, 4b.)
A high level girdle of The Boss.
1) 50ft. Start as for Sunset, climb directly across the slab to a belay 15ft. from the top of Matins.
2) 70ft. Move out right above the lip of the overhang to a good foothold on the edge. Move on to the slab, then cross it to a good spike. Pendulum from the spike to Nail File. Descend slightly to belay.
3) 30ft. Finish as for Party Line.

A good expedition, but needs good rope work and a competent second.

Nail File   60ft.   Hard V.S. (5b)   *
Climb the overhanging cracks immediately right of The Boss. A fine route.

Party Line   60ft.   Hard Severe (4b)
Climb the short corner 15ft. right of Nail File. Move left into a junction with Nail File, then climb diagonally right over a bracket to another ledge. Climb straight up to the top. The best route of its grade on the crag.

Plexor   50ft.   Hard V.S. (5b)
Climb the easy corner to the wide crack splitting the overhang and gain a small ledge over this, with difficulty. Finish up the sandy corner above.

Stump Corner   40ft.   V. Diff.
Climb the steep slab a few feet right of Plexor. Climb to a ledge below a short corner, climb this to an awkward exit.

Stump Crack   30ft.   Diff.
An obvious crack a few feet right of Stump Corner.

NORTH FACE

This is the area of the crag to the right of the central watercourse.

Routon Ridge   40ft.   V. Diff.
Start 30ft. right of the watercourse on the left flank of the ridge. Climb a thin crack past a tree to a good stance. Move leftwards to an incline which is climbed on small holds.

Birch Wall   40ft.   Severe
Start on the right flank of the ridge. Ledges lead diagonally right to a slab. Traverse left to a groove and up this to the top.

Dead Wood Slabs   35ft.   Severe
Same start as Birch Wall, climb the lower slab on small holds, then climb the upper slab on the right.

Skateboard   30ft.   V.S. (4c)
Climbs the slab and left arete of the slab left of Skaters' Corner. A fine route with poor protection.

Skaters' Corner   30ft.   Hard Severe (4b)
Climb the obvious corner 20ft. right of Dead Wood Slabs. Often greasy. Finish on the left.

BEACON BUTTRESS

The prominent buttress towards the right end of the North Face.

Excavator   35ft.   Diff.
Climb the chossy groove line 20ft. left of Gehenna.

Variation Start   15ft.   Hard V.S. (5b)
Climb the finger crack into the groove, often sandy. Best finish; climb down.

INGLEBY ARNCLIFFE AREA

Gehenna   40ft.   Hard V.S. (5a)   ***
Follows the obvious crack splitting the smooth wall on the left of the buttress. Strenuous but well protected. One of the best routes in North Yorkshire.

Beacon Buttress   45ft.   Hard V.S. (5a)   *
Round the corner from Gehenna is a slab below an impending corner. Climb this and the corner to a small ledge, then swing round the corner on to another ledge on the right and finish with difficulty. A fine route.

Direct Finish   Hard V.S.   (5a)
Same as above, but continue up the groove (doubtful flakes).

Epicentre   40ft.   E3 (6a)
Start left of Tremor, just right of Beacon Buttress. Initial protection is in the flake of Tremor. Climb the slab until moves rightwards gain a small pocket just left of the arete. Pull up on to a small resting foothold. Continue diagonally leftwards up the hanging slab to a small ledge below the lefthand of two grooves. Finish up this. This route can be started by climbing Tremor initially, reducing the standard to 5b.

Tremor   40ft.   E2 (5b)   *
Start in an alcove 10ft. right of Beacon Buttress. Climb the crack system at the lefthand side of the alcove direct to the top. Strenuous. A superb route.

Green Wall   35ft.   V.S. (4c)
Climb the groove forming the right side of the alcove on to a slab. Follow the cracks running diagonally right to the top. A good route.

The Groove   35ft.   Hard Severe (4b)
Start in a groove 12ft. right of Green Wall. Climb the groove to bulging rock. Step left then back right to follow cracks to the top.

Solo Wall   30ft.   Hard V.S. (5c)
Start 5ft. right of The Groove. Climb the leaning wall with difficulty, until the angle eases. A hard problem.

WORM HILL BUTTRESS

The isolated buttress beyond the right end of the North Face. It carries several obvious routes. On the extreme left is Helter Skelter an easy but pleasant slab climb.

SCARTH WOOD PINNACLE

An interesting needle problem (35ft. Diff.) can be visited en route to Beacon Scar, by following the stone wall from the top of Shepherd's Hill to a gate set obliquely in the wall. Pass through the gate into the wood where the pinnacle can be found.

98 PEAK SCAR

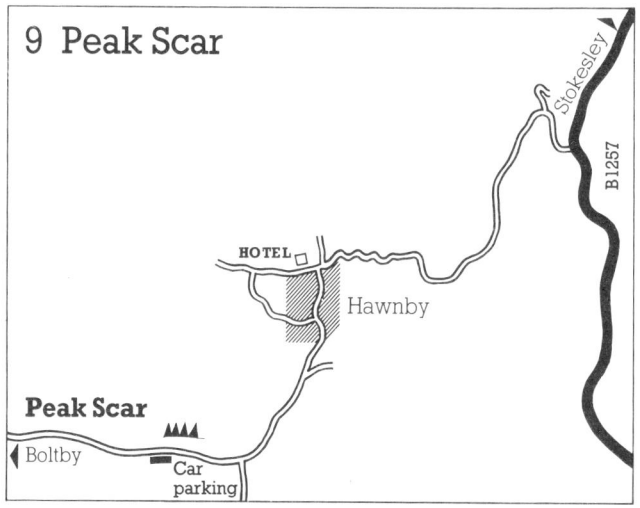

Peak Scar
G.R. 527884

Peak Scar is a limestone cliff near Hawnby. It extends without a break for about 300 yds. and reaches a maximum height of 90ft. The climbing is steep, sometimes strenuous and some routes are quite exposed. With a reasonable selection of modern equipment most climbs can be adequately protected.

The crag faces north and for part of its length it forms one side of a gorge. This, combined with shelter from surrounding trees, often makes the cliff worth a visit when more exposed crags in the area are out of condition.

The crag is divided naturally into three sections, the East Wall, the Main Wall and the West Wall. The East Wall runs from the left end to a point where the line of cliffs comes forward about 10ft. and the gorge narrows. In the corner at this point is Pemba Chimney. The projecting Main Wall, about 300ft. long, extends to a large corner containing the entrance to a cave (Murton Cave). The whole of the right-hand part of the crag beyond the cave is the West Wall.

Like most limestone the rock needs careful treatment in places but generally it is clean and reliable. On a few climbs, especially at either end of the crag, vegetation can be a problem.

HISTORY

The first major contributions to the climbing at Peak Scar were in 1961 by Terry Sullivan, who with Vic Tosh, climbed over thirty routes on the crag, the most notable being Frenesi.

The following year Chris Woodhall repeated all the existing climbs and proceeded to add his own routes such as Trad, Fifi, Milestones Direct, and the imposing Astronaught.

In 1964 Ken Jackson pushed standards higher with the bold Cosmonaut Direct. The following year Chris Woodhall and Stuart Patterson climbed Bivi using two pegs.

During 1968 members of the York M.C. produced a high level girdle, later extended by Tony Marr, who, with John Chadwick also made a free ascent of Crackers, one of the best routes on the crag.

In September 1982 John Redhead and Chris Shorter eliminated four points of aid from BBC to produce one of the hardest climbs at Peak Scar.

APPROACH

Follow the Hawnby to Boltby road for about two miles. Just before point 859 (on the map) is a small gate in the fence on the north side of the road. Pass through the gate and descend, to the left, into the gorge.

There is ample car parking space by the roadside.

EAST WALL

About 30 yards from the left-hand end of the crag the path passes through a gap between two lines of mossy boulders. The vegetated buttress to the left of these contains several routes of various grades but the first listed climb is on the buttress to the right.

1. Sidewinder 40ft. V. Diff.
Start 8ft. from the edge of the buttress. Climb the crack to a ledge. Continue up the crack above.

2. Jonas 40ft. V. Diff.
Start on the same buttress and 10ft. right of Sidewinder. Follow a crack diagonally right to a large ledge. Pull up between two large and slightly overhanging blocks to a stance. Continue up a large bracket on the right and finish directly above.

3. Webar 30ft. Severe
Start in a small corner about 20ft. right of Jonas. Climb the small corner and bulge followed by a crack, to the right, in the overhang. A grassy gully to finish.

At the edge of this buttress is a corner crack with a small narrow cave at its base.

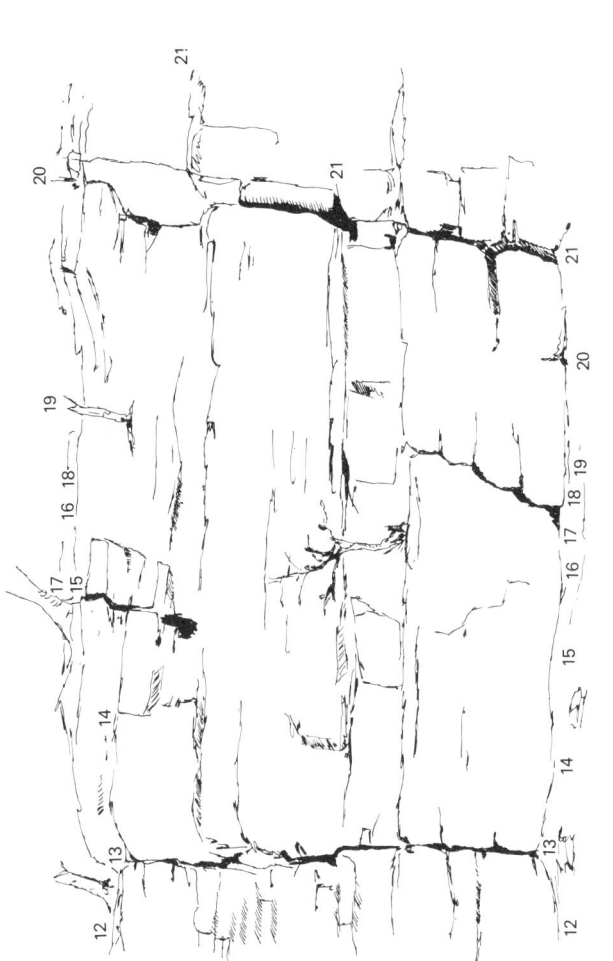

PEAK SCAR – EAST WALL

4. Primo   50ft.   V. Diff.
Start just to the right of the cave. Just above ground level traverse right on to the front of the crag. About 8ft. from the edge climb up to a ledge. Continue up a short wall to a cleft and finish on the right near an oak tree.

5. Womble   50ft.   V.S. (4b)
Start 15ft. right of Primo beneath a large overhang. Climb the obvious corner, moving diagonally right to a crack at the right-hand side of the roof. Climb the crack to gain the ledge above. Follow the continuation of the crack to the top.

6. Trundle   40ft.   Diff.
Start 20ft. right of Womble at the top of the debris cone. Climb up just right of a block forming a small corner. Gain the wall above and climb to the ledge. Climb the wall to the left of a dirty gully.

7. J.C.B.   45ft.   V. Diff.
Start 8ft. right of Trundle. Climb a series of blocks leading left-wards to an obvious ledge. Climb the crack and chimney above.

8. Orinoco   45ft.   Severe
Start at the same place as J.C.B. below a steep thin crack. Climb the crack to a sentry box on the right. Gain the block on the left: a high step and slab lead to the final chimney.

Just beyond the last climb the floor of the gorge levels out. At this point a short dummy wall is set against the crag.

9. Twilight   60ft.   Hard Severe (4b)
Start at the foot of the dummy wall. Climb the wall to the ledge. Climb the thin crack above until forced left up another crack. Move left again and then up a vegetated hollow just below the top. Exit by a short and similarly vegetated crack on the left.

10. Moaning   60ft.   Hard Severe (4b)   *
Start as for the previous climb at the foot of the dummy wall. Climb the wall to a ledge. Move up the short wall and then across right to the foot of a groove. Climb the groove, over a roof, and continue to a tree belay at the top.

11. Kant   70ft.   Hard V.S. (5b)
Climb the faint crack between Moaning and Dat Der. The route follows a direct line over the overhangs.

12. Dat Der   65ft.   V.S. (4c)   *

Starts about 20ft. right of the end of the dummy wall and just left of a vee break in the overhang. Climb up to and through the vee groove to a ledge. Continue up a short wall which is followed by an overhanging crack. Step left and climb the crack in the final overhang. (An easier alternative is to move right before climbing the final overhang.)

13. Jordu   75ft.   Severe   *

An obvious vertical crack line to the right of Dat Der.

14. Fifi   75ft.   Hard V.S. (5a)   *

Start 5ft. right of Jordu. The climb takes a direct line to the left of the prominent overhang at the top of the crag. Climb the short steep wall to a ledge. Climb the corner and pull up over the roof. Continue up a series of short cracks by bridging. Move up and over the next overhang and past loose blocks to a tree at the top.

Variation: From the first ledge climb the corner then move right and finish up the wall just to the left of Pianississimo.

15. Fortissimo   75ft.   Hard V.S. (5b)

Climb the wall and groove between Fifi and Pianississimo. The roof at the top is climbed by a faint groove.

16. Pianississimo   75ft.   V.S. (4b)   *

Starts 25ft. right of Jordu, beneath a prominent flake (The Battleship). Climb the wall on delicate holds, moving to the left at first and then up to the ledge. Climb up and over the overhang above using The Battleship. Continue up the wall and then a short chimney to a tree belay.

17. Ackers   80ft.   V.S. (4c)

Starts 10ft. right of Pianississimo. Climb the wall to a groove which cuts the overhang. Move up through the groove, passing the overhang and continue the line of the crack to the top.

18. Ornithology   90ft.   Severe

Start at some flakes about 20ft. right of Pianississimo. Climb the flakes and traverse left to an elm growing from the wall. Use the tree to climb the overhang and continue up diagonally left to the base of the chimney on Pianississimo. Climb this to the top.

19. Kestrel   80ft.   Hard V.S. (5a)

Start at the same place as Ornithology. Climb up to the ledge on Ornithology. From the right hand end of the ledge climb a niche in the overhang, making an awkward move on to another ledge. Traverse 10ft. left and climb up to a tree at the top.

20. Odds On   75ft.   Hard V.S. (5a)
Climb the wall to the left of Pemba Chimney to a ledge. Climb the overhang at a point 15ft. to the left of the chimney. Move up using two horizontal cracks, make a long reach for a small hold and then move up on ''big jugs'' to the next ledge. Climb the cracks directly above to the top.

Variation: From the first ledge, climb the crack directly above.

MAIN WALL

21. Pemba Chimney   80ft.   Diff.
Start in the corner where the East Wall meets the projecting Main Wall. Climb the wide chimney-crack for 30ft. to a large ledge. An awkward move leads to a fissure beneath two wedged blocks. Continue over easy rocks on the right to a corner and finish up the rather awkward rocks above.

22. Concorde   80ft.   V. Diff.
Start just right of Pemba Chimney. Traverse round to the front of the Main Wall and then up to a ledge. Continue diagonally right to a ledge and finish up the gully.

23. Main Wall   90ft.   Severe
Start 20ft. right of the edge of the Main Wall. Climb the short wall to a ledge. Continue up a fault passing over several doubtful overhanging blocks to a grass ledge. Finish up the chimney above.

24. Weedy Wall   90ft.   Hard V.S. (5a)
Start at a flake 35ft. right of the left edge of the Main Wall. Climb the flake and step right below a short crack. Continue up this, over a bulge and up to a ledge. At the back of the ledge is a large block which tilts downwards below a roof. Climb over the block and roof to finish at a tree.

25. Birdland Eliminate   90ft.   V.S. (4b)
Start beneath a short crack containing flakes about 12ft. right of Weedy Wall. Climb the crack to a ledge. Continue up a thin crack over an overhanging block and continue to another ledge. Climb the overhang and crack directly above and finish, up the corner crack of Birdland.

26. Wings   90ft.   Severe   *
Start at a rock platform 35ft. right of Weedy Wall and 10ft. left of a big roof at the top of the crag. Climb straight up by a series of ledges to a large ledge at 30ft. Move right, along the ledge to a block and then up to gain a wall beneath the canopy. Pass the overhang by a short crack on its right, leading to a recess. Finish the climb up the exposed rocks to the left.

PEAK SCAR – MAIN WALL

PEAK SCAR   105

27. Birdland   90ft.   Severe
Start right of Wings at a rock platform immediately beneath the prominent overhang at the top of the wall. Climb to a ledge at 30ft. by way of a short but stiff corner crack. From the left end of the ledge climb up and left to another ledge. Continue up the walls and corners above to finish at a hawthorn bush.

28. Birdland Direct   90ft.   Hard Severe (4b)   *
Climb the first pitch of Birdland. Above the ledge, climb a sinuous crack in the corner to the left of the large overhang. The crack leads to the top.

To the right of Birdland the gorge reaches its lowest point and the crag its maximum height. Elm trees border the right of this hollow and above is a prominent vertical crack line (Jam with Sam).

29. Zig-Zag   90ft.   Hard V.S. (4c)
Starts at a corner 20ft. left of Jam with Sam. Climb the corner for 10ft., move left under the overhang and mantleshelf on to a wide ledge. Move right from the ledge and hand traverse into a sentry box. Move right again and then climb the vertical wall until the broad ledge on Jam with Sam is reached. Move left up a short wall and then surmount the overhang on good holds.

Direct start. Start just right of the normal route where a thin crack splits the roof beneath the sentry box. Climb the crack and enter the sentry box with difficulty. Use another thin crack to leave the sentry box and continue to join the normal route at the ledge on Jam with Sam.

30. B.B.C.   100ft.   E2 (5c)
Start as for Zig Zag. Climb the thin overhanging crack passing over two roofs to a ledge (5a). Move left until below the overhanging buttress. Climb the roof at its left side and continue directly up the front of the buttress (5c).

The next four climb start from a ledge about 20ft. above the lowest point of the crag.

31. Crackers   100ft.   E2 (5b)
Start 6ft. left of Jam with Sam. Climb the wall to a horizontal crack. Make a long reach for small holds and gain a ledge with difficulty. Move left to below a prominent roof by a protruding block. Climb past the block and round the exposed corner to the left (junction with B.B.C.) Finish directly to the top.

32. Jam with Sam   90ft.   V.S. (4b)
Climb the prominent vertical crack line.

33. Perdido   90ft.   V.S. (4b)
Start just to the right of Jam with Sam. Climb an awkward corner to the left of a small overhang. Move right past a loose flake on to a grass ledge. Continue up the wall, bearing slightly left of protruding rocks past a small ash tree on to a broad ledge. From the ledge climb the wall above to the top.

34. Perdido variation   90ft.   Hard V.S. (5a)
Start as for Perdido. Climb the small corner and bear leftward to a smooth wall. Climb the thin crack and small roof to gain a shallow depression running directly up the wall. Continue up a short wall to gain the final crack in the outer wall of Jam with Sam.

35. Headache Crack   90ft.   V.S. (4c)
Takes the obvious curving crack 15ft. right of Perdido. Climb the crack and make an awkward mantleshelf on to a ledge. Climb straight over some large wedged blocks on to a spacious ledge. Finish up Perdido or climb the small overhanging prow.

36. Pardon   90ft.   V.S. (4b)
Start mid-way between Headache Crack and the groove of Gone. Climb the wall to a ledge. Climb behind a prominent nose of rock and gain its tip. Climb the crack above to a second ledge and then continue up the final crack.

37. Gone   90ft.   Hard Severe (4b)   *
Start at the foot of the groove behind the elm trees. Climb the groove to a ledge above the break in the overhang. Continue up the corner or up the wall to the left of the corner.

38. Male Menopause   90ft.   Hard V.S. (5a)
The arete to the right of Gone is climbed direct.

39. Milestones Super Direct   90ft.   Hard V.S. (5a)
Start just right of Gone. Climb the wall to the ledge below the roof. Climb the roof where two cracks form a ''V'' shape and continue up the wall above passing between two large blocks to a small ledge on the left. Finish up a short crack to the right.

40. Milestones Direct   90ft.   Hard V.S. (5a)
As for Milestones Super Direct until above the roof. Trend right and finish up the last pitch of Milestones.

41. Milestones   90ft.   V.S. (4c)
Start about 15ft. right of Gone at the foot of a large semi-detached flake with a tree growing behind it. Climb the edge of the flake to its apex. Surmount the overhang via a break in the roof. Move right and climb the wall to a narrow ledge. Traverse left to a jammed block. Move up the wall to a wide crack and climb this to finish on the right.

42. Trad   90ft.   Hard V.S. (5a)
Start about 20ft. beyond the elm trees and a few feet left of Downbeat. Step off a large block and climb the bulging wall for a few feet then move left until the overhang is reached. Traverse left to a large thread runner and a step in the overhang above. Gain the wall above and climb to a narrow ledge. Pull over the roof on to the wall on small but good holds and exit by a small chimney to the left.

43. Trad Direct   90ft.   Hard V.S. (5a)
Start just right of Milestones. Climb up to the roof and then move right to join the ordinary route at the thread.

44. Frenesi   90ft.   V.S. (4c)   **
Start at the same place as Trad. Step off the block and climb the bulging wall to a ledge. Surmount the overhang at the vertical crack and move up and diagonally left to a narrow ledge. From the right-hand end of the ledge pull out over the bulge, thin at first but then on good holds. Continue up the wall to the top.

45. Fringe Benefits   90ft.   Hard V.S. (5a)
Start adjacent to Downbeat. Climb directly up the edge of this section of the crag.

46. Downbeat   70ft.   V. Diff.
The obvious chimney/corner crack 30ft. right of the elms.

47. Walking   70ft.   Hard V. Diff.
Start at the foot of a crack 10ft. right of Downbeat. Ascend the zig-zag crack for 15ft. and then up the right-hand edge of protruding rocks. Step out left and finish up a corner just to the left of a large overhang.

48. The Edge   80ft.   V.S. (4c)
Keep as near as possible to the right-hand edge of the Main Wall. Start in the cave at the foot of the edge. Squirm up the crack in the roof to reach a ledge a few feet right of Walking. Climb the flake on the wall until it is possible to traverse right to the edge. Move round the corner and up the wall to a small grass ledge. Continue up the edge to an ivy covered wall. Climb this for a few feet, then traverse left to a nose which is climbed to the top.

49. Frustration   70ft.   V.S. (4c)
Start just to the right of The Edge. Two starts can be made.
1.   Climb the chimney crack and pull over the bulge.
2.   Climb the wall just to the right of the chimney crack and move left.

Continue up the crack until a small ledge is reached then move slightly left and climb the wall to the top past an ivy wall.

50. Solitude 70ft. Severe *
The prominent stepped crack line to the right of Frustration.

51. Murton Cave 50ft. Mod.
Start in the corner where the Main Wall meets the West Wall. Climb up the rocks to the entrance of the cave. Climb the right wall of the cave by devious routes to the exit funnel in the roof. An amusing route and a fairly quick means of descent.

52. Cobweb 50ft. V. Diff.
Start as for Murton Cave. The route runs up the outside of the cave. Climb to the mouth of the cave. Climb the crack on the right wall to an opening. Continue up the corner, well above the cave entrance, to the top of the crag.

WEST WALL

53. Mother Bear 70ft. Hard V.S. (5b)
The wall to the left of Cosmonaut Direct is climbed direct.

54. Cosmonaut 70ft. V.S. (4c) *
Start 10ft. right of Murton Cave. Climb to a broad ledge at 20ft. Follow the series of thin vertical cracks up the wall to the overhang. Move left directly under the ash tree. Using a good hold behind the overhanging bulge pull up and climb to the tree.

55. Cosmonaut Direct 70ft. Hard V.S. (5a) **
Start as for the ordinary route but leave the ledge directly beneath the ash tree near the top of the crag and climb the difficult wall (poorly protected) to the overhang. Surmount the overhang on good holds and continue to the tree.

56. Evasion 70ft. Severe
Start just to the right of Cosmonaut at the foot of an obvious crack. Climb the crack to a ledge. Move up to a grass ledge and continue up the crack to a sentry box. Climb up for six feet and then traverse right to the exit.

Variation start: Hard V.S. (5b)
Climb the bulging rocks, a few feet right of the normal route, to the grassy ledge.

57. Centipede 60ft. Severe
Start 20ft. to the right of Evasion at a shallow cave. Climb the wall on the left of the cave until progress is stopped by poised blocks. Move left and climb the corner to a ledge and traverse right to regain the crack, which is climbed to the top.

PEAK SCAR

58. Marsupial 70ft. V.S. (4b)
Start just right of Centipede by the prominent tree. Climb the tree to gain a ledge on the wall. Move slightly left climb a corner and continue diagonally right to a grass ledge. Continue up the final crack to the top.

59. The Brood 60ft. E2 (5b)
Originally called Inflation, the name of this climb was changed when the points of aid were eliminated. Start 15ft. right of Centipede, underneath a large roof. Climb up to and over the roof (5b). Climb the wall to a flake. Move left on to the wall and climb between the saplings to finish via a crack at the top.

60. Char Paray 70ft. Mild V.S. (4b)
Start 10ft. right of The Brood where a thin crack splits the roof. Climb up to, and using the thin crack, over the roof. A long reach is useful.

61. Deflation 70ft. Severe
Start at the lowest point of the rocks on the West Wall, about 20ft. right of Centipede. Climb to a good ledge at 30ft. Traverse horizontally left for about 10ft. to the foot of a crack. Move up and with difficulty squeeze into the open base of a chimney. A chockstone forces a detour to the right for 10ft. after which the line of the chimney is regained and followed to the top.

62. West Chimney 70ft. V. Diff.
The prominent chimney 30ft. right of the start of Deflation. Scramble up for 25ft. to the base of the chimney. Climb the left wall for 15ft. and then bridge up to some large blocks. Finish up a narrow continuation of the same chimney.

63. Bivy 60ft. E3 (6a)
Takes the prominent roofs at about 10ft. right of the chimney on the previous climb. Scramble to the ledge under the overhang. Climb a crack in a groove and traverse left when stopped by the first roof. Move up and over the next roof with difficulty originally with two pegs but now free. Continue up the wall on the right to the top.

64. Astronaut 70ft. Hard V.S. (5a) *
Start just to the right of Bivy. Make an awkward move up the wall to gain the obvious overhanging corner crack which is followed to the top.

65. West Wall Route 70ft. Mild V.S. (4b)
Start 10ft. right of Astronaut. Climb the overlap on to a small slab and then climb a short corner to a grass ledge. Continue up the wall above to finish up the dirty corner on the right.

66. Dis Here 70ft. V.S. (4c)

Start at a large flake 20ft. right of Astronaut. (Best reached by traversing above the trees). Climb the flake, step out left, and then climb straight up the wall to a small sentry box. Traverse left to a corner, passing a tree, and finish up the vegetation.

67. Davy Jones Locker 50ft. Diff.

Start 50ft. right of West Chimney. Climb a series of ledges to the foot of a wall. Continue diagonally right to the top.

68. Palmsun Chimney 35ft. Mod.

Start 60ft. from the right end of crag, just to the left of a small cave, and about 30ft. right of the last climb. Scramble up to the base of the chimney. Climb the chimney and exit on the left.

69. Palmsun Wall 35ft. V. Diff.

Start just to the right of the cave mentioned above. Climb awkward rocks to a broad ledge. Climb the wall just to the right of the chimney to a narrow ledge. Continue up the broken wall above.

70. Mulligan Mania 400ft. Severe

Start as for Twilight and Moaning at the foot of a dummy wall.

1. 30ft. Climb the dummy wall to the ledge.
2. 30ft. Traverse right to reach Jordu.
3. 35ft. Continue to the elm tree on Ornithology.
4. 25ft. Traverse into Pemba Chimney.
5. 50ft. Cross the chimney and move on to the front of the Main Wall. Continue diagonally right to a grass ledge on Concorde.
6. 70ft. Move easily along the ledge and finally descend to the large ledge on Birdland and Wings.
7. 45ft. Traverse right below the huge canopy, and climb up to the large platform on Jam with Sam.
8. 30ft. Traverse round to the front of the crag on to a good ledge which leads to another corner (Gone).
9. 40ft. Descend Gone for about 5ft. until a traverse line leads right beneath some jammed blocks. Continue to a narrow ledge.
10. 45ft. Continue at the same level, cross Downbeat and finish by way of an ivy corner to a projecting grass ledge.

PEAK SCAR

71. High Level Traverse 650ft. V.S. (4c)

The route originally started at the same place as Mulligan Mania but has since been extended. The additional section starts about 15 yds. from the left end of the crag adjacent to an ivy shrouded corner.

1. 70ft. From the corner cross the wall to a muddy ledge in a corner.
2. 60ft. Climb on to the front of the crag to gain the obvious ledge which crosses Sidewinder and Jonas. Follow this to the next corner.
3. 35ft. Continue at the same height across an awkward wall to join Primo at the cleft. Climb diagonally right to gain the nose of the overhanging prow. Traverse the prow and step down to join Womble.
4. 55ft. Walk along the ledge leading to the sentry box on Orinoco and continue to join Moaning just below the roof.
5. 35ft. Traverse round the nose to join Jordu.
6. 60ft. Traverse rightwards at a constant level to a large ledge in a corner (Odds On).
7. 100ft. Descend slightly to avoid a corner. Step up and cross a grass ledge to another corner. Traverse downwards to a grass ledge and continue at the same level to a large corner (Birdland Direct).
8. 40ft. 4c Traverse round the exposed nose and make a difficult move into an overhung corner (junction with Wings). Continue rightwards to the large platform near the top of Jam with Sam.
9. 30ft. Move on to the front of the crag and traverse to another corner (Gone).
10. 40ft. Descend Gone for about 5ft. until a traverse line leads right beneath some jammed blocks. Continue to a narrow ledge.
11. 80ft. 4b Traverse right at the same level for 45ft. to The Edge. Step up and traverse the wall to a small cave opening (Murton Cave).
12. 30ft. Traverse the steep wall just above a small roof to a sentry box (Evasion).
13. 20ft. Climb the steep crack above then step right and scramble to the top.

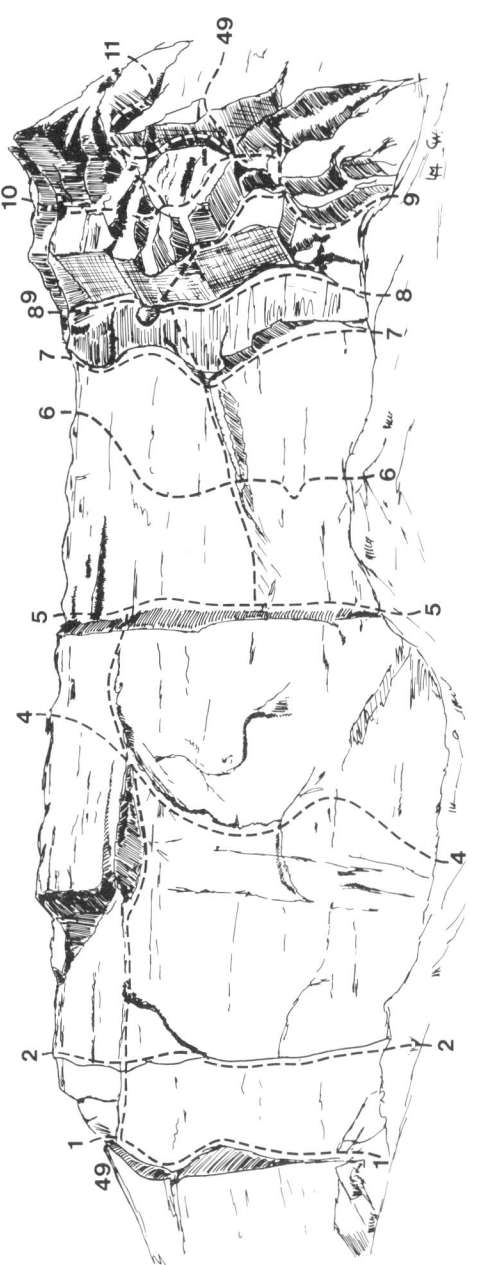

WHITESTONECLIFFE

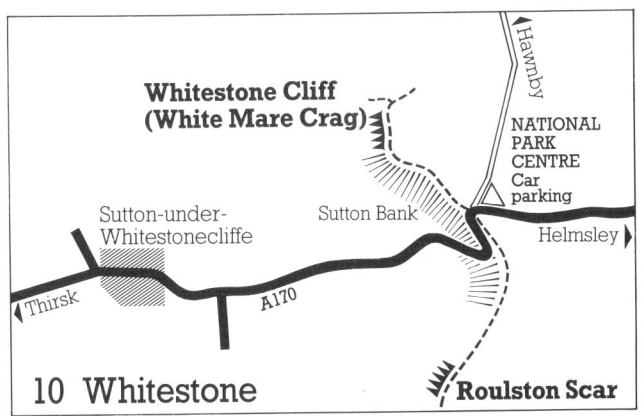

Whitestonecliffe

G.R. 506835

Size, situation and quality of climbing make Whitestonecliffe the major outcrop in the area covered by this volume.

The cliff is reported to have been formed in the early eighteenth century when the steep scarp slope above Sutton village slipped, exposing a continuous outcrop of cretaceous grit over 1000ft. in length and ranging from 50 to 110ft. in height.

The rock is soft but rough and has regular and distinct bedding planes with many horizontal ledges often overhung by roofs. Steep cracks run vertically up the faces.

Weathering has given much of the rock a knobbly formation, providing many sharp but often dubious holds. Rock falls have occurred in recent years, changing the nature of some climbs and deterring many climoers. But for those who enjoy steep exposed climbing on dry sunny walls, with splendid panoramic views of the Vale of York, this cliff will not be a disappointment.

When climbing on Whitestonecliffe, it is suggested that two ropes should be carried as many of the belays are from trees, some way back from the face. It should also be noted that, due to the friable nature of the rock, pegs may not necessarily be in place as stated or they may be in poor condition as a result of corrosion.

HISTORY

Whitestonecliffe was largely ignored until the late 1950's when climbers stationed at the nearby R.A.F. Leeming and Topcliffe pioneered some of the more obvious weaknesses. The real exploration began early in the next decade when members of the Cleveland Mountaineering Club led by Terry Sullivan, enthused by experiences in the Dolomites, ascended two of the best lines, Nightwatch and Countdown on their first visit. C. Woodall, E. Shield and R. Cornwell followed with their ambitious Girdle Traverse, vastly extending the scree but also opening the way for a host of new routes helped by Patterson, Vanmeerbeck, Clarke and many others.

Pitons were used freely in the unstable rock but now most routes have been cleaned and protection devices have improved, so most climbs are led free. To date, most of the climbing is strenuous but not technical. Large areas of compact rock remain unclimbed but it remains to be seen whether the small fragile holds will support or deter the assaults of the new wave of cragsmen.

ACCESS

The cliff is clearly visible to travellers on the A1 and A19 but should not be confused with its more southerly neighbour Roulston Scar which lies adjacent to the famous White Horse.

Cars can be parked at the National Park Centre at the top of Sutton Bank on the A170. The well trodden Cleveland Way path is followed north west for half a mile until the top of the cliff is reached. Care should be observed in descending. An obvious gully cuts the cliff close to its southern end but this can be dangerous if wet and the safest descent is down steep grass with a short scramble at the extreme North end of the cliff. The land below the cliffs is under the care of the Nature Conservancy and although it is crossed by Nature Trails no paths exist up to the base of the cliff. As interesting flora and fauna survive in the seclusion of the dense wood and briar, attempts to reach the cliff should not be made from this direction.

1. Masochist   40ft.   Severe

The climb starts up the first chimney crack approximately 30ft. from the left hand end. Climb the crack and with difficulty gain a ledge on the left. Climb the final bulge to the top.

2. Conflict   65ft.   V.S. (4c)

Starts 15ft. to the right of Masochist and follows the crack line running parallel to Masochist.

    40ft.   Climb the crack for 20ft. on to a small ledge then with difficulty move up using the crack for hand jams. Move on to the large flake on the right (peg belay).

    25ft.   Regain the crack and move up to the bulge on to large hand holds and then by the short crack to the top.

WHITESTONECLIFFE 115

3. Couldn't Again   90ft.   Hard V.S. (5a)
The climb uses a new start to the direct finish of Couldn't, a climb which once existed but which was demolished by a rock fall.
Starts beneath the obvious shield of rock a few feet right of Conflict.
> 50ft. Climb to the flake and ascend the right corner crack of the flake to its top. Cross the Girdle Traverse and climb rightwards to a small stance and bolt belay.
> 40ft. From the belay climb the overhanging groove on the right.

4. Throwback   90ft.   V.S. (4c)
Starts at a faint corner 15ft. to the right of the original start to Couldn't below a small tree half-way up the crag.
> 80ft. The corner crack or adjacent wall is climbed to a small ledge. From the ledge move left under a large, loose flake to a tree. The crack behind the tree is climbed to a small ledge. From the ledge make an awkward move right to a gangway. Belay a few feet back.
> 20ft. Follow the gangway right until an obvious line leads to the top.

5. Pygmalion   100ft.   Hard Severe (4b)
The start lies 30ft. to the right of Throwback up a large open corner with a crack in the back. This is one of the prominent corners of the crag. The route is serious for the grade.

Climb the wall on the right on good holds until an awkward move at 60ft. is made to gain a small ledge. The wall on the left is climbed until a bulge is reached. This is climbed on the left using small holds for a few feet and then large holds appear at the top.

6. Wailing Wall   100ft.   Hard V.S. A1
Starts 20ft. right of Pygmalion.
> 60ft. Start in the centre of the wall moving left after 30ft. to reach a ledge. Move diagonally left again before the obvious traverse right is made to the centre of the wall and peg belay. Poor rock. Two or three protection pegs are necessary.
> 40ft. Climb the inverted 'V' slab above (protection peg), step right and climb the steepening wall with the aid of two pegs. Swing right again to escape near the top of Last Post.

7. Last Post   100ft.   V.S. (4b)
Starts 40ft. right of Pygmalion up the first obvious crack from the last climb. Climb the wall for 6ft. until the crack is reached, using hand jams. Move up until a step left can be made on to a belay ledge. Follow the gangway up and make an awkward move out over a bulge to the top.

WHITESTONECLIFFE

WHITESTONECLIFFE 117

8. Clutcher   100ft.   V.S. (4c)   *

Starts round the corner from Last Post and is the prominent chimney running up the left hand side of the large overhangs. The first few feet are climbed on the outside of the crack and then the best method of attack is to climb with your right arm and leg in the crack until a set of perched blocks is reached. Either climb over or under the blocks to reach a chimney crack which is then climbed to the top.

Just to the right of Clutcher is a prominent overhanging buttress. Three lines are easily distinguished, the first being Blitzkreig which takes a faint crack line starting up to the left and finishing up Clutcher. The second is Espeekay which cuts through the middle of the buttress and the third is Black Mamba which skirts the right hand side.

9. Blitzkreig   110ft.   Severe A2   *

Starts 15ft. to the right of Clutcher.
- 40ft. Climb the crack for 30ft. to reach the cave and ledges below the roofs.
- 50ft. Traverse left under the first roof and then move up to the left. Follow the crack line to a small roof and traverse left on to a stance (Clutcher).
- 20ft. Finish up the top of Clutcher.

10. Espeekay   100ft.   V.S. (4c) A1   **

Starts at the crack line directly below the right hand side of the cave.
- 40ft. Climb the crack to the cave belay.
- 60ft. From the cave climb left beneath the roofs to reach a groove. Follow the obvious line to the top.

11. Black Mamba   120ft.   E2 (5b)   ***

- 40ft. As for Espeekay.
- 40ft. The thin crack at the back of the large ledge and just to the left of the traversing line (Chameleon) is climbed, followed by difficult climbing to the obvious roof. The roof is taken on the left, followed by very exposed climbing round the corner on the right, past loose blocks to a comfortable stance.
- 40ft. Move slightly down and to the right to climb a short steep crack and then up to a large crack and the top.

12. The Possum   110ft.   V.S. (4c) A2

Start 20ft. right of the main overhangs.
- 60ft. Peg the wall, then move left and over a small roof past a bolt. Follow the crack until two more bolts are reached, then move right and up the crack to a good ledge. Belay on the right.
- 50ft. Climb the crack to another ledge, then traverse left round a corner and up a loose crack, past a flake to the top. Seldom climbed.

A through route has been done following roughly the line of the climb.

13. Ying and Yang   90ft.   Hard V.S. (5b)   ***
Start 40ft. right of the main overhangs.
> 60ft. Climb a short chimney crack to the left of a detached block. From the block step on to the slab and move up to the overhangs. Move left, pass beneath the overhang and gain the wall above. Climb the wall until another overhang is reached. Move left for 5ft. and climb the overhang. Move up awkwardly to gain the ledge. Belay.
>
> 30ft. Move right and climb the steep wall to the top.

14. Sassenach   110ft.   V.S. (5a)   *
This climb is getting progressively looser. One of the first lines on the crag to be climbed. Starts just right of Ying and Yang.
> 80ft. Surmount the large detached block and the sloping ledge with ease. Make a difficult traverse right until a hand jam high up is reached. Pull up and traverse slightly left, then straight up to a stance.
>
> 30ft. Traverse right, then straight up a narrow crack followed by another traverse to a ledge. Climb the crack to the top.

15. Gamin   65ft.   Severe
Start at the corner chimney crack to the right of Sassenach. Climb the chimney until a chockstone is reached, then move out right and up the wall to a tree belay.

16. Pillar of Winds   200ft.   Hard V.S. (5b)
A high level traverse of the Ying and Yang Wall. Technically not extreme but a sustained and serious route with poor rock.

Start as for Gamin.
> 60ft. Climb Gamin to the tree.
>
> 80ft. Step up on the left and traverse horizontally left along the obvious line for 35ft. to a peg. Move down and left on to a small ledge. Continue left and upwards slightly on side pulls. Gain a ledge on the left with difficulty and continue left to Ying and Yang descending this to the stance.
>
> 60ft. Traverse left along the ledge (pegs for protection) to gain a small ledge on the Possum.
>
> Traverse left along the ledge to the foot of a crack (Black Mamba). Protection pegs. Climb the crack to the top. The rock on this pitch is poor.

17. Yangtze   65ft.   Severe (4b)
Starts just right of Gamin.

Climb up to a ledge on the arete. Continue more or less up the arete to the top.

18. Thyrus 60ft. Severe

Start round the corner on the right behind a large boulder which almost leans against the face. Climb the groove making use of several small pocket holds until a small ledge is reached. Either continue up the crack above or more left on small holds and move up the wall on to the slab and continue to the top.

19. The Leash 110ft. V.S. (4c) *

Starts 15ft. right of Thyrus below the large slab.

    80ft. Climb the wall using a thin crack, then move slightly left using a large flake and gain a small ledge. Move right on to a slab and then up to a steep wall. Climb the wall on good holds and reach the large slab. Cross the slab to the left and belay beneath the black overhanging crack.

    30ft. Climb the crack (loose) and move out on to the overhang on excellent holds and continue to the top.

20. Double Time 90ft. V.S. (4b)

Starts 30ft. right of The Leash, to the right of a huge block and below the right hand end of the large slab.

    40ft. Climb the obvious crack line to the slab. Peg belay.

    50ft. Move straight up the wall and step right into a small chimney. Move left and then right to another chimney (peg for protection). Finish up on the right on very loose rubble.

This route is not recommended.

21. Garbage Groove 80ft. Diff.

Starts 30ft. right of the last climb. Its main interest lies in its novel start which is a natural rock bridge over a crevasse. Cross the bridge and climb the chimney to the top.

22. The Trembler 120ft. V.S. (4c)

    60ft. Climb the groove moving out right below a roof to gain a grass ledge (peg belay).

    60ft. Step left and climb a crack past a small sapling. Traverse right until standing on a huge detached block (seen from below). Move upwards and rightwards to finish on grass.

23. Garth's Causeway 80ft. V. Diff.

Round the corner on the right lie twin cracks, the one on the left being chocked by a tree. Climb the right hand crack to a ledge. Pull up left to gain a second ledge above the tree of the left hand groove (or climb the left hand groove). Not very pleasant. Straight on up the narrow chimney on good holds, which is enjoyable until the chimney leans slightly and narrows to a crack. Good holds are available for a pull over however, or one can make an even easier ascent up the left hand wall.

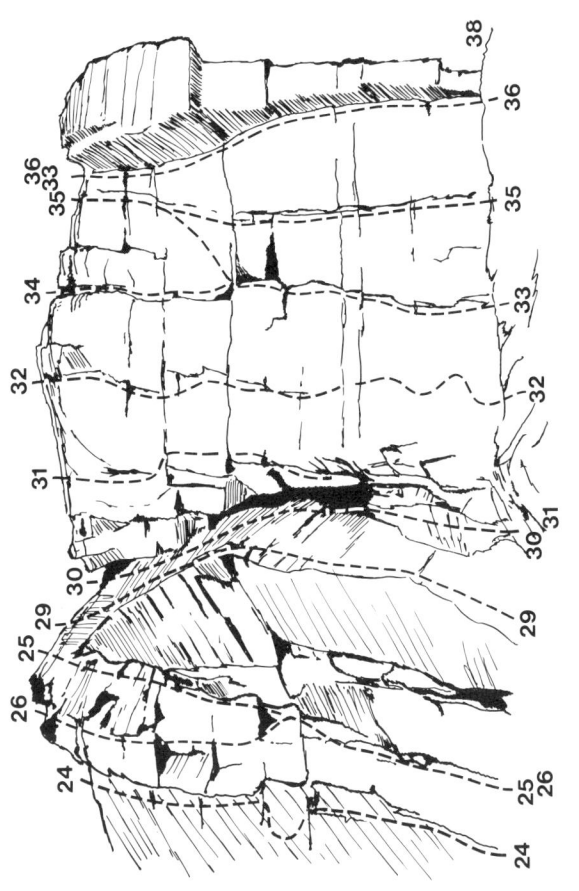

WHITESTONECLIFFE

WHITESTONECLIFFE 121

24. The Nocker   90ft.   V.S. (5a)
Start at a corner 10ft. right of Garth's Causeway.
    30ft. Climb the corner to a large grass ledge.
    60ft. Step right and climb up to the overhang. Move up past this and on to the top.

25. Odin   100ft.   Severe (4b)   *
One of the first lines on the crag to be climbed. It is deservedly one of the most popular routes.

Starts 10ft. right of The Nocker at the foot of some twin cracks.
    30ft. Climb the twin cracks to a small ledge and tree belay.
    70ft. Straight up on small holds above the belay to a prominent flake, then to a small bay below the final overhanging crack which is the crux. Facing left, jam up and over the bulge on shattered blocks to a small ledge and then scramble to the top. (Usually done as a one-pitch climb).

26. Odin Direct   70ft.   Hard V.S. (5a) A2
Start from the tree belay at the top of pitch one of Odin. Climb a steep corner to the left of the crack of Odin to the roof. Over the roof by a crack on the right (pegs).

27. Frigg   130ft.   Hard Severe (4b)   **
Start a few feet right of Odin at the foot of a long corner. Climb the corner crack and continue to a small overhang at 60ft. A few feet above the overhang a ledge leads out right to the arete up which the climb finishes.

28. Mars Bar   150ft.   V.S. (5a)
Start about 4ft. right of Frigg. Climb the wall for 50ft. to a small ledge. Climb up to a roof which is surmounted with the aid of a piton. Place a second piton below the next roof and climb strenuously over this to the top.

29. Pie and Pea Pillar   150ft.   Hard V.S. (5a)
The overhanging arete between Odin and Gauche.
    30ft. Start on the right of the arete and climb to a sandy overhang. Pull up and move left onto the edge. Traverse right then up the wall to a peg belay on the corner.
    70ft. Start on the left of the ledge, then move round to the right of the arete to a thread. Straight up the bulging wall and continue up the easy slab to the top where the line joins Odin.

29a. A route with some artificial aid has been done to the right of Pie and Pea Pillar. The rock is poor but escape is always feasible on the left or right to more obvious lines.

30. Gauche 70ft. V. Diff.
30ft to the right of Pie and Pea Pillar is a large chimney with huge ceilings. The start is up the rib of rock that divides the lower half into two chimneys. One of the most pleasant routes on the crag.
- 30ft. Up the rib to a choice of belays in the cave.
- 40ft. Climb up the back of the cave and then move left on excellent holds until past the ceilings. Straight on up to the top.

31. The Skab 110ft. Hard V.S. (5a)
- 30ft. Same start as Gauche i.e. climb the rib to the ledge.
- 80ft. Climb the grooves to the right of the cave (crux), pull out into the crack above and then traverse left to a flaked crack which is jammed. Continue up steep, loose rock to the top.

32. The Claw 110ft. E4 (5c) *
Starts 15ft right of Gauche, to the left of Countdown.

Climb the wall and mantleshelf onto a small ledge. Step right, then left again to reach the parallel horizontal cracks of Chameleon. Climb a thin crack to reach a large incut ledge with a tree stump. The final moves are hard.

Climb past an old protection peg on small holds to a small roof where some thread runners may be placed. Swing strenuously left and up to more broken but still steep rocks above, leading to the top.

33. Countdown 150ft. Hard V.S. (5a)
The first prominent crack to the right of The Claw.
- 55ft. Climb the wall and crack, passing an awkward bulge and mantleshelf onto a ledge.
- 50ft. Traverse right along a ledge to a centre crack. Climb this, trending right until the final overhang is reached. Step right to finish at the top.

34. Countdown Direct 100ft. V.S. (4c) **
- 55ft. First pitch of Countdown.
- 45ft. From the ledge step left and follow the crack which is a continuation of the crack line of Pitch 1.

  This is a more satisfying finish to the original line of Countdown.

35. Central Crack 110ft. Hard V.S. (5a) **
Starts to the right of Countdown and follows another prominent crack line.
- 55ft. Climb the crack to a ledge, passing a bulge with difficulty.
- 55ft. Continue the crack to the top.

36. Nightwatch   110ft.   Hard Severe (4b)   ***
The impressive chimney/crackline just right of Central Crack. This is one of the outstanding routes of the crag, and the best limestone severe in the area. Climb the crack throughout. A fine line in a good situation offering steep but well-protected climbing.

37. Bad Concept   110ft.   Hard V.S. (5b) A2
This route follows the steep overhang capped prow to the right of Nightwatch. Strenuous free climbing eventually gives way to pitons and bolts some of which were removed in a recent rockfall.

It is doubtful if this climb has been repeated since the rockfall. The original grading has been given.

38. Gormire Eliminate   110ft.   Hard V.S. (5b) A2
Start in the groove 10ft. right of Nightwatch.

It is unlikely that this climb has, to date, been repeated since a recent rockfall at 70ft.
- 60ft. The groove gives 50ft. of good climbing. A belay can be arranged on a sloping ledge.
- 50ft. Step up left into a capped groove. Some poor threads and pegs are used to ascend the steep wall above.

39. Backache Crack   85ft.   V.S. (4b)
Takes the next corner.
- 45ft. Climb the crack for 30ft., then move left onto a small ledge. Peg belay.
- 40ft. Climb the crack in the corner and bridge over the overhang to a small tree. Belay just below the top.

40. Absinthe   65ft.   Severe (4b)
The start lies up a thin crack to the right of an elderberry bush about 15ft. right of Backache Crack. Climb the crack, move right, then up a wall on the left until stopped by a bulge. Move right round a corner to a tree. Belay.

The crag is now split by a large grass gully, sometimes used as a descent gully. On the right of the gully the crag gradually tapers down.

41. Domino   50ft.   V.S. (4c)
Climb the crack to the right of the gully, taking care of loose blocks near the top. Move right a few feet from the top to a tree belay. Scramble to the top.

42. One Half Shift   50ft.   V.S. (4c)
Climb the crack right of Domino. Pass a bulge at 20ft., then a short wall and finish up the groove above to a tree belay.

43. Hobbledehoy   50ft.   Severe
Just to the right of the previous climb, a prominent crack line leads to a shallow bay at 40ft. Take the steep crack on good holds to the shallow bay. Climb the crack on the right of the ivy, to the top. A good introductory route to the crag.

44. Ace of Hearts   50ft.   V. Diff.
To the right of Hobbledehoy is a well-defined chimney. Climb this, taking care on the last few feet to avoid loose blocks.

45. Confusion   45ft.   Severe
Round the next corner a square block stands at the foot of a large curving crack. From the block, climb the wall with the aid of the crack until stopped by the overhanging blocks. Move left and up to a tree belay.

46. Finesse   45ft.   Severe
20ft. right of the last climb, another chimney cuts the buttress (Humdrum). Just to the left, a crack line winds its way to the top.

47. Humdrum   35ft.   V. Diff.
Just to the right of the previous climb is a chimney. This is climbed on good holds.

48. Penumbra   35ft.   Diff.
Round the corner lies another chimney. This is climbed, moving left near to the top.

To the right lies a gully-cum-chimney which provides an easy, moderate standard, descent route.

49. Chameleon 880ft. Hard V.S. A2

This is a traverse of the cliff. Although first completed by traversing from left to right the most interesting situations can be experienced by tackling the route from right to left.

Starts at the south end of the main crag in the descent gully.

1. 30ft. 4b Traverse leftwards across the broken wall to belay in the large corner of Backache Crack.
2. 60ft. 4c Cross the steep wall to a good stance on Gormire Eliminate at 60ft. height. Continue to a narrow ledge on the prow. Step into Nightwatch and descend 20ft. to belay in the chimney at 40ft. level.
3. 55ft. 4c Follow the obvious crack by hand traverse to reach a ledge and first belay of Gauche.
4. 75ft. 4c Cross the wall to the rib and continue more easily on broken ledges to an old tree left of Odin. Traverse to a grass ledge leading to the next corner.
5. 25ft. 4b Cross the steep wall above the tree to reach Garbage Groove. Belay.
6. 60ft. 4c Move round the next corner and down to a narrow ledge to reach a crack leading to a stance before the large slab.
7. 60ft. 4b Cross the slab on sandy holds. Peg for protection not in place. Belay on better rock on the Leash.
8. 20ft. 4a Step down and round a corner to tree belays.
9. 40ft. 4a Climb Thyrus and step onto a tree belay at the top of Gamin.
10. 50ft. Abseil from the tree to a ledge about 20ft. from the ground.
11. 110 ft. 4c Continue across the obvious line of ledges, interrupted by a corner on Ying and Yang. Some in situ pegs offer protection on the steep wall before reaching an exposed peg belay on the extreme edge of the buttress.
12. 20ft. A1 Step down and round the corner (pegs in place) to reach an excellent cave.
13. 70ft. A2 Follow pitch 2 of Blitzkreig to the blocks on Clutcher. Make an exposed move across the wall to Last Post (thread belay).
14. 50ft. 4b Descend the grassy gangway of Last Post to a ledge system crossing Wailing Wall to the large corner of Pygmalion.
15. 35ft. 4c Climb the corner of Pygmalion to a grassy ledge below the cliff top.

16. 60ft. 5a   Descend the grass ledges which form the top of Throwback to reach a steep strenuous traverse below small overhangs leading to the bolt belay of Couldn't Again.

17. 60ft. 4c   Continue the line to complete the traverse at the top of Masochist.

ROULSTON SCAR   G.R. 511815

This scar is very prominent in the view looking south from the top of Sutton Bank where it borders the Gliding Ground. It is 300 yards long and up to 100ft. high. Many routes have been climbed but due to the very friable nature of the rock none are described.

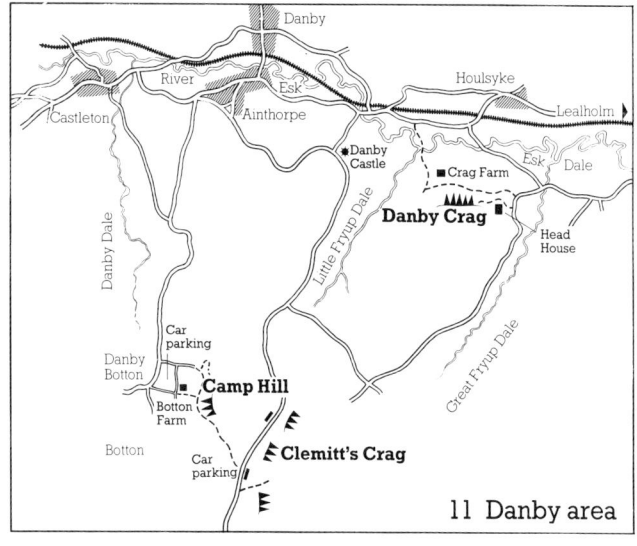

11 Danby area

Eskdale Area

DANBY CRAG G.R. 730068

HISTORY

The crag's development was poineered by John Jackson and Terry Sullivan who climbed Valiant and Vulcan, but it then lay dormant for many years. Early in 1974 members of the Northumberland Mountaineering Club paid a number of visits climbing twenty new routes, among them George Mitcheson's Osiris and Hugh Banner's Isis.

APPROACH

Proceed about a mile beyond Danby on the road to Lealholm, taking the Houlskye road and turn down the approach to Crag Farm. Note -there is no vehicular access beyond the bridge over the Esk. On foot, follow the track to the woods. The crag occupies the escarpment in the woods above the farm. From this point, the crag runs towards the east for about half a mile; the extreme west corner is joined to the main rocks by a narrow band of broken rock.

Alternatively, follow signs towards Fryup until a sharp bend is reached below Head House. The path leads past Head House and along the top of the crag.

The area below the crag is thickly wooded and the traverse along the bottom of the crag involves negotiating an area of large fallen blocks, and care should be taken.

The routes are described from right to left.

NORTH WEST BUTTRESS

The isolated buttress at the western end of the escarpment nearest to Danby Village.

Castle Chimney 30ft. Diff.
Start at the right edge of the buttress. Climb the chimney over wedged blocks.

Castle Ridge 30ft. V. Diff.
Six feet left of Castle Chimney is a wall. Climb to a horizontal crack and continue up the ridge above.

Mood Indigo 30ft. V. Diff.
Start round the corner, 20ft. left of the last climb. Climb the groove to a ledge. Finish up the twin cracks.

ESKDALE AREA

Broken Chimney   30ft.   Diff.
Start 5ft. left of Mood Indigo, at the lowest point of the buttress. Climb the left bulge direct to finish up the chimney.

Birch Crack   20ft.   V. Diff.
Climb the crack with a Birch in it 10ft. left of the last climb.
 A girdle traverse can be made of the North West Buttress at V. Diff. Start as for Castle Ridge and finish up Birch Crack.

Forty yards to the left of Birch Crack is a broken face of rocks. There are several climbs recorded here.

Bracken Corner   20ft.   Diff.
Start to the right of a projection. Scrambling leads to a ledge occupied by a large clump of bracken. Climb the slanting crack on the left wall.

Genevieve   20ft.   Diff.
Start 6ft left of Bracken Corner. Climb to a recess and finish either side of a u-shaped tree.

Wraith   20ft.   V. Diff.
Start as for Genevieve. Finish up narrow slab.

Phantom   20ft.   Diff.
Start 15ft. left of Genevieve. Enter a cave and squirm up the back until it is possible to emerge onto the face.

Twisting Chimney   20ft.   V. Diff.
Start 6ft left of Phantom. From a large block step right onto the buttress and climb direct to the top.

Fifty yards left brings one to a ravine. About 10 yds. inside the right-hand entrance to the ravine is:-

Vulcan   25ft.   V.S. (4c)
Start right of a leaning heap of boulders. Climb the impressive corner crack.

Grasshopper   25ft.   Diff.
Climbs a grassy crack just left of Vulcan.

Thrutch   25ft.   Severe
Start in a corner 10 yds. left of Vulcan. Climb the crack.

Nemesis   30ft.   V.S. (4c)
Start at the corner left of Thrutch. Climb the left side of the arete until it is possible to gain a small corner on the arete up which the climb finishes.

Creeper Wall   40ft.   V. Diff.
Start in a hollow at the lowest part of the ravine. Climb the angled crack to a stance and follow more broken rocks to the top.

Little Greenhopper   25ft.   V. Diff.
Start 15ft. left of Creeper Wall. Climb the short crack and then the groove to the top.

The left entrance of the ravine is here and the first climb outside it is:-

Silo   30ft.   Hard Severe (4b)
Start 5ft. left of the last climb. Climb the obvious thin crack running up the wall. Escapeable but good climbing.

Tendril   25ft.   V. Diff.
Start to the right of a rib 20ft. left of the ravine. Climb to a protruding block, then follow the crack.

Scrabble   20ft.   V. Diff.
Start just left of Tendril. Climb the crack, tree and chimney.

Across the grass rake stands a fine buttress with a holly tree springing from a ledge on the left.

BEACON BUTTRESS

Chimney and Wall   30ft.   Severe
Start from the right flank of Beacon Buttress at a small chimney. Climb the chimney to a wedged flake. Step left, gain a ledge and finish up a crack on the ridge.

Valiant   30ft.   V.S. (4c)
The groove 10ft. left of Chimney and Wall. Surmount the bulge and climb the awkward groove above. A good climb.

Beacon Groove   30ft.   Diff.
Start left of Valiant at an Ash. Scramble up to a tree and follow the groove to the top.

Sodom   30ft.   Severe
Start left of Beacon Groove. Climb a steep crack and narrow chimney line.

Gommorah   30ft.   Severe
The obvious fist-width crack just left of Sodom.

Venom   35ft.   Severe
Start below a holly tree 15ft. left of Beacon Groove. Climb the crack to the holly. Climb the crack on the left and ascend the overhang on the right.

Beacon Chimney   35ft.   Severe
Six feet left of Venom. Climb to a recess, then the wall on the right to the chimney, which is followed to the top.

The next two routes are on the back wall of the recess, bounding the right-hand side of Owl Buttress.

Ninevah   30ft.   Hard Severe (4b)
The corner crack - extremely wet.

Babylon   30ft.   Severe
The ramp which slopes left into the wide crack, 10ft. left of Ninevah.

OWL BUTTRESS

The obvious, smooth-looking buttress.

Bastile   25ft.   Severe
The corner crack on the flank of Owl Buttress.

Tawny Cracks   30ft.   Diff.
Start 10ft. in from the right-hand end of the buttress at an s-shaped crack. Climb this using the slab to aid progress.

Pygmy   30ft.   V. Diff.
The crack and corner left of Tawny Cracks.

Portcullis   20ft.   V.S. (5a)
Start just left of Pygmy. Climb the wide crack set in a shallow corner.

Turret Crack   25ft.   V.S. (4c)
The narrow 'v' groove and jamming crack left of Portcullis.

Battlement   25ft.   Severe
The crack up the left side of Owl Buttress, alongside a pinnacle.

Snowy   25ft.   Diff.
Start at the foot of Owl Chimney. Climb the right wall, move right and then directly to the top.

Owl Chimney   20ft.   Diff.
The deeply-cut cleft on the left flank of Owl Buttress. Enter the chimney and climb a crack on the right.

ESKDALE AREA

Southern Comfort 25ft. Hard Severe (4b)
The steep corner 25ft. left of Owl Chimney.

Poseidon 25ft. Hard Severe (4b)
Start 15ft. left of the last route. Climb a triangular slab and the narrow chimney above.

Horus 25ft. Hard Severe (4b)
A jamming crack formed by the right edge of a huge flake 5ft. left of Poseidon.

Set 25ft. Mild V.S. (4b)
A crack on the left side of Horus' flake.

Minute Man 25ft. Hard Severe (4b)
Just to the left of Set. Climb a slab to an overhanging recess which is quitted using a hold on the right arete.

Damp Squib 25ft. V. Diff.
Start 10ft. left of Minute Man. Climb to the right of an arete. Finish up a crack to a tree.

The next route lies in the prominent corner 10 yds. left.

Roosevelt 25ft. V.S. (4c)
The obvious curving crack line and concave slab. Climb the crack and move right to finish.

Winston 20ft. Severe
Climb the crack in the next prominent corner.

Slime Crack 20ft. Severe
Start left of Winston and immediately right of a spring which drips over the rocks. Climb the crack. Unpleasant.

Left of the watercourse is:-

RADAR BUTTRESS

Osiris 35ft. Hard V.S. (5a)
The crooked jamming crack up the front of the buttress is climbed. A sustained route.

Isis 35ft. Hard V.S. (5b)
Start 6ft. left of Osiris. A difficult finger crack running up the left, past a small tree, to the top of the buttress.

Gee 65ft. V.S. (4c)
Start 10ft. in from the right of the buttress and about 30ft. from the spring. Climb a greasy corner for 25ft. to a grassy ledge. Continue up an open gully for 15ft. and enter the final groove which leads to the top.

Dewline 65ft. V.S. (4c)
Start to the left of Gee. Climb the cleaned buttress by a thin crack in its nose to a grassy ledge. Climb the thin crack into the corner finishing to the right into Gee.

7K 65ft. V.S. (4c)
Start 10ft. left of Gee below a Rowan tree. Climb straight up past the Rowan to a grass ledge. Easy climbing leads to a ledge and a crack at its left end; climb this and the groove above to the top.

Twenty feet to the left is a gully/chimney containing a large protruding flake:-

Aerial Gully 60ft. V. Diff.
Climb a rib for 30ft. to the foot of the gully. Continue for 15ft. to the protruding flake. Move left up the wall until a step back right onto the flake can be made. Finish up a broken wall on the left. A good route.

Prickly Chimney 40ft. Diff.
Ten feet left of Aerial Gully, but at a higher level. Climb through the Holly to a chimney then up this. Unpleasant.

A hundred yards further left from Prickley Chimney is a large, two-tier buttress with an overhanging chimney.

Outrigger 40ft. Severe
Climb the chimney.

Left of Outrigger lies a section of the crag attaining about 20ft. Many lines are possible on here.

About 200 yds. left of the last buttress is a buttress containing a wedge below a roof, above which grows a twisted Oak. The following climbs start there.

Gardener's World 30ft. V.S. (4c)
Climb the corner beneath the roof. Exit left and climb to the top.

Green Corner 30ft. Severe
Start just left of Gardener's World. Climb the corner throughout.

Elder Groove 25ft. Diff.
Start 20ft. left of Green Corner behind an Elderberry bush. Climb the groove.

ESKDALE AREA 133

CLEMITTS CRAG   G.R. 709037

The crags face south-east and are spread over a mile length of hillside. The best faces are 40ft. high and of compact sandstone. The main crag is reasonably clean and dry; however, other buttresses are little frequented and are more vegetated.

HISTORY

The crag was discovered by members of the C.M.C., including C. Woodall, R. Clarke and P. Goodwin, who added Yellow Brick Road. Later development is credited in particular to A. Moss together with K. Neal and N. Dixon. Routes on the north right-hand buttress are principally by S. Brown and D. Paul.

APPROACH

Follow the main Eskdale road east (towards Danby) out of Castleton. 200 yds. outside the village just over a small bridge turn right to Ainthorpe. From Ainthorpe take the most main road right up to Little Fryup Dale. At the head of the Dale the road bends left into Great Fryup Dale. A minor road labelled "unsuitable for motors" goes off right and up a bank out of the valley and on to the moor. Follow this road for a mile until on a very slight bend leftwards, then a grass layby should be seen. Park here and walk left (east) for 400 yards along a path to a stone wall - the path crosses the wall by a gate and descends the hillside. Continue on the path for 200 yards to the foot of the hill and turn northwards along a path at the foot of the hillside - Clemitts Crag will shortly come into view on the lefthand side. Alternatively approach from the stone wall that runs above the crag.

MAIN CRAG

The Main Crag has a massive roof at the right-hand end of the crag.

Box Crack   40ft.   V.S. (4c)
20ft. right of the left arete of the buttress are twin cracks in the head wall guarded by a box chimney below. Climb up the chimney and cracks.

Choke Chimney   40ft.   Severe
15ft. right of Box Crack. Climb the chimney to the top past a holly tree.

Variant   Severe
Climb up the obvious slab and crack right of Choke Chimney.

Period Pains   30ft.   V.S. (5a)
Climb the vertical crack 7ft. right of Rainy Day Blues.

Rainy Day Blues   35ft.   E1 (5c)
Climb the obvious thin crack up the bulging wall behind the bushy tree.
A fine problem.

Buck up Your Ideas   30ft.   Hard V.S. (5b)
Climb the groove 20ft. right of Rainy Day Blues.

Capstone Chimney   40ft.   Diff.
Climb the obvious green chimney capped by a roof. A variant on the
right has been climbed into the chimney.

Yellow Brick Road   45ft.   Hard V.S. (4c)
Start 5ft. right of the chimney. Climb up and right to the arete just below
the roof. Move right, round the arete and so to the top. A good bold
route.

HIDDEN BUTTRESS

100ft. below the Main Buttress is an obvious path traversing the hillside.
Follow the path south (left, facing the crag), for 250 yds. The path rises
and passes a large grassy buttress, the right-hand buttress. 50ft. left of
this is Touch of Class Buttress, and 50ft. left of this buttress is the Left-
hand Buttress, characterised by the sharp arete. There is considerable
vegetation on and around both buttresses.

LEFT-HAND BUTTRESS

Choss Crack   35ft.   Diff.
Climb the slabby crack on the left, passing a tree.

Monkeyhanger   35ft.   V.S. (4c)
Start below a prominent groove capped by a small roof at 10ft. Pass the
roof on either the left or right-hand side and climb up the groove to the
tree.

Apes or Ballerinas   35ft.   Hard V.S. (5b)
Climb the prominent left arete of the chimney direct.

Vee Chimney   35ft.   V. Diff.
Climb the obvious chimney on the right-hand side of the crag.

TOUCH OF CLASS BUTTRESS

This is characterised by a small roof at two-thirds height, running into a
diagonal break starting at the bottom of the crag.

Limelight   40ft.   Hard V.S. (5a)
Start on the left. Climb rightwards up the slab past an in situ thread to the break. Traverse left for 10ft. then finish via a tree filled crack.

Touch of Class   40ft.   E2 (5c)
Start 10ft. left of Variety Show. Climb the slab leftwards to the roof, climb over the roof via a crack and ledge to the top. A fine climb.

Variety Show   40ft.   E2 (5b)
An excellent, bold climb. Climb the obvious lefthand flake/break to the roof, climb over this and so to the top.

If You Like It.   35ft.   Hard V.S. (5b)
Climb the flakey wall to the break at 15ft., move left and up the wall, finishing just right of a prominent tree.

Flakey Wall   35ft.   V.S. (4c)
Climb flakes on the left wall of the chimney.

Unnamed   35ft.   Diff.
Climb the chimney on the right.

12th Night   130ft.   Hard V.S. (5a)
1. Start 10ft. right of the chimney. Climb up and left to belay in the chimney.
2. Traverse left to If You Like It, then into Variety Show, and along the break finishing up Limelight.

Toad in The Hole   50ft.   Hard V.S. (5a)
Start just left of the centre of the buttress, 40ft. right of Flakey Wall. Climb the slabby groove to the bulge, move right into an exposed position. Make a hard move to gain the crack, then climb the crack to the top past a rotting peg, and finish by an old tree.

CLEMITTS CRAG RIGHTHAND

This is a continuation of Clemitts Crag escarpment. Follow the path below Main Crag northwards for 400 yards - there are several small isolated areas of rock and further on a more continuous stretch of rock on which several routes have been recorded, of which the two below are probably the best. The rock is not clean and appears loose in some areas.

Hulk   25ft.   Hard V.S. (5b)
Start at the chimney on the right of the overhang. Climb left on to the ledge. Using the horizontal slots, reach the arete. Layback the arete to the top.

Blankety Blank   25ft.   Hard V.S. (5b)
Climb the bulge direct from right to left to a ledge. From the ledge climb the sharp arete, just left of a shallow groove.

CAMP HILL
G.R. 702044

A small crag with three buttresses overlooking Botton Hall near the head of Danby Dale.

HISTORY

The crag was discovered in 1976 by C. Woodhall and S. Pattison but nothing was recorded. Later N. Dixon, D. Paul, S. Brown and others climbed and recorded their routes.

APPROACHES

Follow the minor road from either Castleton or Danby up to Danby Dale. Just before Botton Village turn left up a bank and follow this road to its end. The crag can be seen on the moor above.

LEFTHAND BUTTRESS

Original Route   25ft.   Severe
Climb over broken rock and ascend the slab above.

F. All   25ft.   Hard V.S. (5a)
Climbs the left hand arete.

Cling Wrap   25ft.   Hard V.S. (5b)
The obvious flake in the centre of the buttress is reached from the right. Climb this and exit on the right.

Scoop Wall   15ft.   Severe
Climb the scoop to the right of Cling Wrap.

MAIN BUTTRESS

This is the large central buttress of the crag.

Tempest   20ft.   V.S. (5a)
Climb the left wall. Long reaches are an advantage.

Jester   20ft.   Hard V.S. (5b)
10ft. right of the blunt arete of Tempest is an obvious green groove. Climb this moving left at the top.

Ace of Winds   30ft.   Hard V.S. (5b)
In the centre of the buttress is a thin flake-crack. Climb this and the wall above. Climb directly through the roof at the top. An excellent route.

Waves Within 30ft. E3 (6a)
Climbs the wall right of Ace of Winds. Start just right of a flake. Climb the wall past a ledge, moving up using a pocket. Finish via a crack in the overhang.

Deceptive Benders 45ft. Hard V.S. (5a)
A girdle of the main buttress. Start by climbing Tempest to the move below the top. Move right below the roofs to reach Ace of Winds. Continue moving right to gain a crack. Climb this to the top.

Ordinary Route 30ft. V.S. (4c)
15ft. right of Ace of Winds are two cracks. Climb the right-hand crack to a large ledge. Climb the slab on the left to finish.

RIGHTHAND BUTTRESS

Flakey Wall 20ft. Hard V.S. (5b)
Climb the bulge on the lefthand side of the wall. Climb up the wall above to finish.

Pickpocket 20ft. Hard V.S. (5b)
Climb the centre of the wall.

Allain's Arete 15ft. Hard V.S. (5c)
The arete just right of Pickpocket is climbed.

30 yards along the moor is a small buttress split by a prominent easy chimney.

Lost Crack 15ft. V.S. (4b)
Climb the obvious crack and groove.

Lost Wall 15ft. V.S. (5a)
Climb the wall right of Lost Crack.

Hookey 15ft. Hard V.S. (5b)
To the left of the chimney climb the lefthand side of the wall via a break and a pocket.

The Arch 15ft. V.S. (5a)
Climb the arch in the centre of the wall.

Silly Arete 15ft. Severe
Climb the arete on the right of the buttress.

ROSEBERRY TOPPING G.R. 579126

The 'Matterhorn of Cleveland' is too prominent a feature of the landscape to require description. It is the site of an ancient settlement and can be reached from quite a number of places, the shortest and most direct being from Newton Under Roseberry near Great Ayton.

The main South-west Face is loose and potentially dangerous. No routes are listed here, though a number of lines have been climbed. Some are apparently sound but suffice to say that care should be exercised when exploring this area.

THE SLAB

This is the name given to the feature lying below the Main Face, and it is quite solid.

Slab Route (ordinary)   35ft.   V. Diff.
Start under an overhang at the base of the slab. Cross a small slab to the right of the corner. Step over a small overhang then move diagonally left to a wide ledge. Finish up the slab above.

Slab Route (direct)   35ft.   V.S. (4c)
Start under a groove in the base of the slab. Climb the groove direct with difficulty to a ledge. Finish up the middle of the slab above.

THE SOUTH-EAST CORNER

Situated to the right of the Main Face on the corner facing Captain Cook's Monument. The rock here is good quality solid sandstone. The climbs are described from left to right.

The Groove   30ft.   Diff.
Start at the south corner. Gain the ledge by the crack, ascend the narrow slab above, the angle of which eases towards the top.

Walla   20ft.   Hard Severe (4b)
Start 5ft. right of the groove. Climb the wall directly passing a series of holds.

Summer House Crack   20ft.   V. Diff.
Start in the corner right of Walla. A short cleft leads to the crack which is climbed direct.

The Mantleshelf   12ft.   V.S. (4c)
Around the corner 10ft. right of the last climb is to be found a curving ledge a few feet up. Gain the ledge and climb to the top.

The Cleft   12ft.   Hard Severe (4b)
Climb the left-hand of two cracks, 5ft. right of the Mantleshelf.

Aireyholme Chimney   15ft.   Diff.
Climb just right of The Cleft.

Neb   15ft.   Severe
Start 5ft. to the right of the last climb. Gain the ledge, then follow the slab above.

The Alcove Left-Hand   12ft.   Hard Diff.
Climb the left-hand corner of the alcove, round the corner from Neb.

The Alcove Right-Hand   12ft.   V. Diff.
The crack to the right of the above route.

Dangle   15ft.   Hard Severe (4b)
Start 10ft. right of the last climb. Gain a horizontal ledge and hand traverse left along the lip of the overhang until it is possible to reach holds leading to the top.
  A direct start can be made at V.S. (4c).

CRINGLE CRAG   G.R. 538033

The crag lies on the north flank of Cringle Moor. From a distance the crag is difficult to recognise because the same hillside contains a number of outcrops. However, at close quarters, the crag cannot be mistaken because of the jutting overhangs at half height. Unfortunately the outcrop is slow to dry and the rock is of dubious quality and lichenous. Belays are difficult to find and in some cases it is safest to belay using an extra rope from the outcrops above.

APPROACHES

The crag is best approached by turning off the A172 into Carlton Village. Pass through the village on the road to Chop Gate and follow Carlton Bank until the road summit is reached. Walk east along the Cleveland Way but instead of taking the path that goes to the summit of Cringle Moor follow the path that contours around the north side. After about a mile the crag can be seen in the lower centre of the concave north side of the hill, approximately 400ft. below the summit.

MAIN CRAG

The crag is split on the left by a grassy gully left of which is a smaller steep buttress.

El Spiderman   35ft.   E1 (5b)
Just right of the centre of this buttress is a groove. Start up this, swing out left and climb the wall and shallow corner to finish.

Walk On By   35ft.   V.S. (4c)
The groove and crack on the right of the buttress.

Right of the gully lies the main buttress.

El Lawrence   45ft.   E3 (5c)
15ft. right of the gully is an obvious groove capped by a roof. Climb this turning the roof on the right.

10ft. right of El Lawrence is an obvious arete.

Cosmic Wipeout   20ft.   Hard V.S. (5a)
Start 5ft. right of El Lawrence. Climb the wall 5ft. left of the arete, traverse right and up as for Cosmic Debris.

The Voice   25ft.   E1 (5b)
Climb the wall just right of the arete, then either left and up El Lawrence, or right and up Cosmic Debris. A good problem.

Cosmic Debris   50ft.   V.S. (5a)
Climbs the obvious corner in the middle of the crag. Starts 10ft. right of The Voice at the left of the alcove. Climb the corner, continue up a crack to a small overhang, turn this on the left, then up to finish.

Terry's Dilemma   60ft.   A2
Climb the initial corner of Cosmic Debris (severe), then gain the hanging groove right of Cosmic Debris.

Wedge Route   55ft.   E4 (6a)
Start at the right hand corner of the alcove. Climb the corner to the roof. Traverse the thin crack rightwards to the lip. Climb direct to the top via an obvious crack system. A good route but usually damp.

Direct Route   50ft.   A3
This takes the thin crack and roof to the right of Wedge Route (3 pegs). The wall above the roof (2 bolts).

Last of a Dying Breed   50ft.   E2 (5c)
Start just right of the huge roof of Direct Route below a sandy corner. Make a difficult move to start, then climb to a rest below the roof. Climb over the roof and up the groove and crack above. A good route.

Every Step of the Way   50ft.   E3 (5c)
Start 15ft. right of Last of a Dying Breed, below an obvious groove. Climb up the groove for 30ft. to an obvious sandy ledge, loose flake. Traverse right beneath the overhangs to a scoop. Swing right on to the arete and up a short groove to the top. A good route.

Crowmagnon   120ft.   E3 5c 5b/c
A girdle of the crag, good climbing. Start at a groove 15ft. left of El Lawrence.
1. 80ft. Climb the groove and sloping groove above peg runner (not in situ) to gain a ledge on the right, peg runner (not in situ). Hand traverse the lip of the roof to gain El Lawrence peg runner. Move right to bolts, right over grass to Terry's Dilemma, traverse the wall descending slightly, swing around the arete into Wedge Route. Belay.
2. 40ft. Climb down rightwards across the green slab to gain ledges. From the right end of the ledges, step down, continue the traverse, feet on top ledge, to gain a shallow groove. Climb the groove to a bolt belay (in situ).

The right outcrop is 100ft. higher on the right of the main outcrop.

Humble Crack   25ft.   E3 (5c)
Climbs the obvious curving crack with an undercut base. A rest can be taken on the ledge on the right side of the arete.

Hank's Route   25ft.   Hard V.S. (5a)
The obvious corner groove 10ft. right of Humble Crack.

On the face opposite and left of Hank's Route is a slabby wall.

Darlo Special   20ft.   Hard Severe (4b)
Climbs the slabby wall. Pleasant climbing, no belay.

The left outcrop is 150ft. higher on the left of the main outcrop.

Sloper   40ft.   V.S. (4c)
Start in the corner under the overhang. Climb the crack to the roof, then hand traverse left and up to the top. Strenuous.

Amigos   20ft.   Hard V.S. (5c)
The obvious crack splitting the overhang on the downslope side of the buttress. To finish traverse left at a grassy ledge.

LOWER FOX CRAG   G.R. 521026

This is the lower of two bands of rock on Carlton Moor, (known locally as Pin Point) lying below point 1338. It is easily reached from the top of Carlton Bank. One route has been recorded.

Busby Crack   30ft.   Diff.
Starts 10 yds. from the left of the crag. Climb the wide crack split by a flake to the top of the buttress.

SILTON CRAGS G.R. 448940

A number of buttresses can be seen on the left of the road approaching Over Silton from the A19. The best approach is to take the forestry road from the north of Over Silton village. On leaving the village, a path leads up to the left by the forestry 'Fire' sign. Follow the path until it reaches a forestry track. 20 yards along the track turn left and follow a fence which leads to the edge of the escarpment. Turn left again and the main buttress is a further 100 yards diagonally downwards. It can be recognized by a fallen tree, the roots of which overhang the end of the buttress and support a precarious boulder. At the left end of the buttress is a forked oak.

Forked Oak Chimney   35ft.   V. Diff.
Follow the chimney immediately behind the tree, taking care of the loose blocks in the middle.

Lost Buttress   35ft.   Severe
Start 6 feet right of the last route at the foot of the buttress. Climb up to a notch and traverse diagonally left to the top.

Knees Up   40ft.   Severe
Just right of Lost Buttress is a gully. Start on the left wall moving across the gully to the right wall and then direct to the top.

Pieman   35ft.   V. Diff.
Climb the chimney direct 6 feet right of Knees Up and around a corner.

To the right of Pieman is an impressive wall overhung at its right hand end.

Simple   40ft.   Hard Severe (4b)
Start at the left end of the wall and climb straight up to a prominent crack which is behind an overhanging tree branch. Climb this to the top.

Simon   40ft.   Severe
Start just right of Simple. Climb the wall on weathered holds. At about two thirds height traverse 6 feet right on to the arete and then climb straight up. A fine route but poor protection.

Around the next corner is an obvious double chimney.

Elderberry Chimney   40ft.   Diff.
Start to the left of the foot of the left-hand branch. Climb behind an elderberry bush into the chimney then direct to the top.

OTHER CRAGS 143

Birds Nest   40ft.   V. Diff.
Start just right of the chimney base. Climb the right-hand branch using the right wall.

20 feet right of the last route is a rather loose slab.

Branch   35ft.   Hard V. Diff.
On the left of the slab is a chimney. Climb this, by-passing the loose central section on the right. Finish up the awkward chimney to the left of the oak with three trunks at the top of the crag.

Silton Stairs   30ft.   Diff.
Start 4 feet right of the last route. Climb up steps on the slab to the top. Avoid the loose middle section on the right.

Across a wide grassy gully is another buttress with a large cave.

Spiney Norman   35ft.   Diff.
Start at the stone embedded in the ground at the foot of the buttress to the left of the cave. Climb on weathered holds until the overhanging wall above stops progress. Traverse left to finish.

35 yards right of the main area are broken buttresses on which a number of routes have been climbed.

KEPWICK CRAG   G.R. 467905

The crag is situated immediately above Kepwick village.

APPROACH

From the A19 follow minor roads towards Kepwick village. Take the second white gate after the house 'Monument View' and follow the track, through another gate, to the crest of the hill to the left of the crag, then back right to the crag.
   The routes are situated in three bays, separated by grass ramps.

LEFTHAND BAY

Kepwick Crack   20ft.   Hard Severe (4a)
The square corner right of a prominent nose.

Leg Slip   15ft.   V.S. (4b)
20 yards right of Kepwick Crack is another nose with a wide crack on its lefthand side. Climb the crack moving right at the top.

Offside   15ft.   Hard Severe (4b)
Climb the alcove to the right of the nose.

RIGHTHAND BAY

The righthand bay is dominated by a large impressive wall. On the right of this are three cracks and a square corner.

Sticky Wicket   35ft.   E1 (5b)
The left-hand crack is climbed.

Maiden Over   35ft.   V.S. (4c)
Climb the wall to the right of Sticky Wicket and continue up the wide crack on the right-hand side. A sustained pitch.

Stumped   35ft.   V.S. (4c)
Another sustained climb. The square corner to the right of Maiden Over is climbed.

Silly Mid On   35ft.   V.S. (4c)
Climbs the arete right of the corner and finishes up the wide crack on the right.

TRANMIRE ROCKS   G.R. 575006

This band of rocks borders the Moor of Broad Ings behind Bilsdale Hall. Leave the main road just before the Chop Gate and, passing through Seave Green, turn right in front of the Hall. This track soon swings up towards the moor and the rocks are reached in 15-20 minutes. At the time of publication there are access problems to this crag.

The crag is about 300 yards long and offers good climbing in a pleasant situation. The first climbs to be found lie on an isolated buttress about 200-300 yards left of the main footpath leading up to the moor top. A plantation of quite large pine trees lie just in front of the crag, separated by a high stone wall.

A prominent buttress capped by a large tree lies in the centre of the outcrop.

Fern Groove   20ft.   Hard V.S. (5a)
The nose forming the left edge of the buttress is split by a shallow groove. The climb follows this direct.

Old Wedge Route   20ft.   Hard V.S. (5b)
To the right of Fern Groove is a short steep wall split by a thin crack. Climb the crack which has an old wedge in place.

Greasy Corner   15ft.   Severe
Climb the corner groove just right of the last climb.

Heather Wall   15ft.   Hard V.S. (5a)
Just right of Greasy Corner, climb the awkward bulging wall.

By following the wall right from the stile two buttresses are found before the main crag is reached. The first buttress consists of a steep wall and a slab before a stream.

Starting from the left edge of the buttress nearest the stile are:-

Banana   10ft.   Hard Severe (4b)
Layback up the buttress 10ft left of a heather filled groove.

Gravity Groove   10ft.   Hard Severe (4b)
Layback the heathery groove on a good edge.

The Ripper   10ft.   Hard V.S. (5a)
15ft. right of Gravity Groove. Bridge up a shallow corner on poor footholds.

On the slab next to the stream are the following routes.

Slab Mantleshelf   15ft.   V. Diff.
Mantleshelf onto a small ledge about 12ft. up and then to the top.

Slab Groove   20ft.   V. Diff.
A groove at mid height is followed to the top.

Slab Edge   20ft.   Diff.
Follows the right edge of the wall on good holds.

70 yards to the right is another buttress formed by two walls separated by a heather slope. The climbs are on the right hand wall.

Linda   25ft.   Mild V.S. (4a)
Start at the left hand end of the undercut base of the wall. Climb over the underdcut base and continue directly up the wall above. An enjoyable route.

Spikey   20ft.   Hard V. Diff.
Start beneath the undercut base, beneath a small overhang 8ft. right of Linda. Climb over the undercut and up the wall above passing the overhang to finish by a small spike. Poor holds to finish.

Long Player   20ft.   Diff.
Start just right of the undercut and climb the slabs at the right edge of the buttress.

Vee   15ft.   Severe
The short wall right of the drystone wall is climbed direct.

Flying   25ft.   V.S. (4c)
Start 8ft. left of Trapeze below a flake. Gain a ledge below an obvious short corner which is climbed to the top.

146   OTHER CRAGS

Trapeze   20ft.   Hard V. Diff.
Start in a niche below a large birch growing from the top of the buttress. Climb the niche for a few feet until it is possible to gain a ledge on the right. Climb direct to finish at tree.

RD's   15ft.   Hard Diff.
Climb the left hand side of the pinnacle right of Trapeze.

Gee Bee   20ft.   V. Diff.
Climb the pinnacle by the crack and arete on its right hand edge.

Approximately 40 yards further right is a small buttress with a prominent 5" wide crack at its left hand end above the jumble of boulders.

Fils Folly   15ft.   Mild Severe
Ascend the slab to the left of the crack using the crack for side holds. Interesting.

Third Degree   15ft.   Severe
Ascend the crack itself, either laybacking or jamming.

Winkers Wall   15ft.   V.S. (4c)
The wall to the right of Third Degree give this awkward climb.

Ramblers Pushover   10ft.   Diff.
The crack to the right of Winkers Wall.

Grumpy   15ft.   Diff.
Starts at the right hand edge of a large block at the left end of the main rocks and 20ft. right of a holly tree. Climb the crack on the right of the block, steep at first to finish left by the stone wall.

Spread Eagle   20ft.   V. Diff.
Start 6ft. right of Grumpy. Ascend a short wall to a ledge continuing straight to the top to finish close by the wall.

Golden Eagle   25ft.   V. Diff.
Start 3ft. right of the last climb. Ascend the short wall to the ledge and continue up a groove to finish by the wall.

Girdle Traverse   150ft.   V.S. (5a)
Start a few feet right of Golden Eagle. Gain a traversing line a few feet up by some difficult moves. The traverse follows an obvious line at an almost constant level. The climb contains some delightful pieces of climbing at a varied standard. On reaching Pluto finish up this climb.

Flake Traverse 30ft. Hard Severe (4b)
Start 14 yards right of Golden Eagle. Mount a short crack to a slab which leads to a flake of rock on a sloping ledge. Traverse 13ft. to the left to a concave wall, climb the wall and gain the top by moving right. A good climb.

Bee Line 25ft. V.S. (4c)
Start as for Flake Traverse but instead of moving left, continue up the crack above to the moor.

Lacuna 25ft. Severe
Start 6 yards right of Flake Traverse and just to the left of an undercut. Climb the steep wall and slab to a crack which is followed to the top.

Tranmire Crack 20ft. Diff.
Start 10ft. right of Lacuna at a small cave. Climb the corner crack to the moor.

Tranmire Groove 20ft. Mod.
Start 10ft. right of Tranmire Crack. The obvious climb running leftwards on broken rocks.

Jupiter 20ft. V.S. (4c)
Start just right of Tranmire Groove, follow the shallow crack running diagonally right. Keep left at the bifurcation. A good route.

Variation Finish 25ft. V.S. (4c)
Start as for Jupiter but keep right at the bifurcation.

Neptune 25ft. Hard V. Diff.
Start at a corner 20ft. right of Jupiter, climb the corner, traverse left into a groove and so to the top.

Pluto 25ft. Hard Severe (4b)
Start 20ft right of Neptune, climb a short wall to the overhang. Make for a nick in the skyline.

Mosque 25ft. V.S. (4c)
Start 5ft. right of Pluto, climb the wall direct.

To the right of this buttress is a short chimney with a chockstone.

Snakes and Ladders 25ft. Hard Severe (4b)
Start at the foot of a buttress 20ft. beyond the chimney. Easy steps to a ledge which is traversed left to a flake. This is the first of three large steps laid against the wall. From the last step an easy finish lies to the left but a more interesting finish is to traverse back onto the wall and so direct to the top. A pleasant climb.

148   OTHER CRAGS

Wedges   25ft.   Hard V.S. (5b)
Lies 30ft. right of Snakes and Ladders. The climb is up a diagonal overhanging crack containing old wedges.

Godiva   20ft.   V. Diff.
Start 15ft. left of the stone wall, ascend any of the three cracks to a large ledge. Climb the wall just to the left of the undercut. A variation start can be made by climbing the crack 8ft. right of the above start.

Oak Tree Crack   20ft.   Severe
Start right of Godiva below an overhanging crack with a small tree at the top. Climb a thin crack in the first wall to the ledge, climb the crack above on good jams.

TRIPSDALE   G.R. 583 987

KAY NEST CRAG

Leave the Stokesley - Helmsley road about a mile beyond Chop Gate and take the track to Cam House Farm. A path then leads over Nab Ridge to the pleasant valley of Tripsdale. The foot of the crag, flanking the eastern side of the valley, is reached in about half an hour.

The crag can also be reached by taking the first lane to the left after Ledge Beck bridge (two miles from Chop Gate) and by walking up Tripsdale after passing through the farms at the foot of the valley. Cars can be taken as far as Hagg House Farm (permission must be asked) for parking. Small numbers only.

There is a good footpath at the top of the crag and this is used in preference to the awkward rocky undergrowth below the crag.

Tally Ho   60ft.   Severe
Lies just to the left of the centre of the main crag. Scramble to a large ledge covered with broom, slabs lead to an open chimney. Move right beneath an overhang to the foot of a short crack. Climb the crack to an oak. Twin cracks lead to the top.

Stirrup Cup   60ft.   V. Diff.
Starts 20 ft. to the right of Tally Ho. Scramble to the base of a chimney. Climb the chimney passing over the chockstones to a broad ledge. Continue up the gully to the top.

Main Face   90ft.   A2 VS (5a)
Start at a holly tree a few feet right of Stirrup Cup.
1. 10ft. (4b). Climb the short wall on the right of the holly tree to a grass ledge.
2. 65ft. A2 (5a). Free climb up and round the corner to gain a line of bolts, in place. Gain a ledge and follow a thin bulging crack (4 pegs). Using a peg in a horizontal crack on the left, move left and climb up to a grassy ledge. Move right to belay at an oak.
3. 15ft. (4a). Climb the crack behind the oak to the moor.

OTHER CRAGS 149

On the next buttress, 200 yards to the right, two routes are recorded, Avalanche Wall and Bonny Face, but these have been obscured due to rockfall and vegetation.

The next climb lies 45ft. to the right, just to the left of a prominent undercut buttress.

Stout Crack   45ft.   V.S. (4c)
Climb the corner crack throughout.

Scout Crack   45ft.   Severe
Starts 3 yds. right of the last climb in a corner. Climb the crack (strenuous). Continue up a gully via a holly tree.

Slanter   20ft.   Severe
Takes the leaning crack 5 yds. right of the last climb. Climb the crack finishing through a tree.

Vee Chimney   20ft.   Severe
Starts 5 yds. right of Slanter. Climb the obvious chimney and protruding block.

Hagg End Ridge   40ft.   Severe
The ridge at the extreme right of the crag. After an awkward undercut start a series of mantleshelves leads to the short wall beneath the top (belay).

Variation   15ft.   Severe
A variation start can be made by a traverse in from the left along a narrow ledge.

OAK CRAG   G.R. 685963

Oak Crag is situated on the east side of Farndale. It is best reached from the Castleton - Hutton le Hole road about 2 miles beyond Blakey House (Low Inn), at the point where a line of shooting butts crosses the road. By walking down the moor, keeping the line of the butts on the left, the rocks are soon found.

NORTH BUTTRESS

This is the isolated buttress on the left, as viewed from below the crags.

Captain Birdseye   25ft.   Hard V.S. (5b)
The slab 2 yds. left of Centre Route.

Centre Route   25ft.   Diff.
Start from the foot of the buttress which protrudes from the middle of the face, and runs straight up it.

Cote Crack   20ft.   Severe
Starts from a recess 10ft. right of Centre Route. A thin crack is climbed to the top.

Rigg Slab   20ft.   Diff.
Starts near the right-hand end of the buttress and takes the slab.

About 75 yds. to the right of North Buttress is:-

BLAKEY RIDGE

Wall and Crack   40ft.   Severe
Starts from a cave at a heap of stones. A strenuous climb out of the cave on to the wall is followed by a crack which is followed throughout.

Blakey Traverse   45ft.   Diff.
Start just round a corner to the right of the last climb. Climb a short wall and then traverse diagonally left to the skyline.

A further 50 yds. south is:-

OAK BUTTRESS

Ash Groove   25ft.   Mod.
Start a few feet in from the left of the buttress and follow the obvious groove.

Ash Tree Wall   30ft.   Diff.
Starts at a cleft just to the right of the groove and runs straight up the wall.

Oak Traverse   45ft.   Diff.
Starts from the cleft, which is climbed. Continue across the wall and finish up a short chimney above.

Oak Wall   40ft.   Diff.
Start just below and right of the oak. Go easily up rocks to the chimney of the last route.

Daffodil Slab   35ft.   Severe
Starts 15ft. right of Oak Wall and runs straight up the slab to a ledge. The wall above the ledge is awkward.

MIDDLE HEAD CRAG G.R. 632011

Developed by Dave Paul and Steve Brown this crag is situated in a pleasant place at the head of Farndale and gives a number of short routes, some of which are very worthwhile.

APPROACHES

May be reached by following the Lyke Wake Walk south-east from Clay Bank car park to Middle Head via Botton Head. The old railway track should be quitted atop the spur of Middle Head from where the crag is gained by walking half a mile to the south. This pleasant stroll takes about 1½ hours. Alternatively approach from the head of Farndale - 20 minutes.

Composed of natural, weathered sandstone the crag can be divided into four buttresses. The rock is generally solid.

MIDDLE HEAD BUTTRESS

Situated roughly in the centre of the crag, it is characterised by a large roof.

Do or Fly   25ft.   Hard V.S. (5c)
Climb a wall and overhang direct 20ft. left of a perched block.

Taboo   25ft.   Hard Severe (4b)
The pleasant corner just left of the perched block.

P.B. left-hand   20ft.   Mod.
The obvious crack/flake on the left-hand side of the perched block.

P.B. right-hand   20ft.   Mod.
A line of ledges which is a useful descent.

Beowulf   30ft.   E2 (5b)
The obvious roof-crack. A fine route of much character.

Rowen   25ft.   V. Diff.
The wall and crack 15ft. right of the roof.

HOLLY BUTTRESS

Para   20ft.   V.S. (5b)
The delicate little scoop on the left edge of the buttress.

Woodstock   20ft.   Severe
The obvious crack up the dark wall; pleasant.

Rock Pipit   30ft.   E1 (5b)
The groove and black overhang via the cleft.

The next buttress is obvious from the name:

THE PROW

Assegai   25ft.   Hard V.S. (5b)
The left wall of the obvious arete.

Zulu   35ft.   Severe
The large, rounded arete. A nice climb.

La fuente del ritmo   35ft.   V.S. (4c)
The right wall of the arete.

Snowflake   25ft.   Hard V.S. (5b)
The arete and corner 30ft. right of Zulu.

Good old mutt.   25ft.   Hard V.S. (5a)
The chossy corner and crack in the overhang left of the Prow.

One man and his dog.   25ft.   Hard V.S. (5a)
The attractive cleft right of the Prow without the aid of the tree.

Choc-a block   25ft.   V. Diff.
Start up One man and his dog. Traverse right around the big block. Finish up a wide crack.

About 100ft. to the right lies:

Iron Men   20ft.   Hard V.S. (5a)
The steep, red wall on small holds.

ESKLETS   G.R. 662020

This outcrop is situated about ½ mile north-east of Esklets Farm and a mile due west of Ralph's Cross. There are two outcrops about 100 yards apart. The most northerly section is referred to as the Crag End Buttress and the southerly as the Main Buttress. There are numerous other short outcrops which provide pleasant bouldering.

APPROACHES

The rocks may be reached from Castleton by walking to Westerdale, following the river Esk, through Wood Dale House and the deserted Pie Thorn Farm. Vehicles may go as far as Waite's House. Alternatively, the road over Castleton Rigg should be taken as far as the well known Ralph's Cross. From here a line across the moor passing close to the lesser known Ralph's Cross West, brings one to the top of the crag in about 25 minutes.

   At the time of publication there are access problems to this crag.

CRAG END BUTTRESS

Crag End Wall 15ft. V. Diff.
The climb lies on the wall immediately south of a tree. Ascend the steep wall on the good holds. (A climb on the right-hand side of the wall can be made at a similar standard).

Bulging Wall 15ft. V. Diff.
Start 10 yds. south-east of the last climb at a corner. Climb the wall bearing right at the first ledge.

Easy Chimney 15ft. Diff.
The chimney 10ft. right of Bulging Wall.

Holly Tree Wall 20ft. Diff.
Start 30ft. right of East Chimney. Climb the slabs to a holly tree and then traverse above the tree. Overgrown and poor.

MAIN BUTTRESS

This buttress provides the finest climbs on sound weathered sandstone.

Dwarf's Ear 20ft. Severe
On a ledge about 5ft. up the face can be seen a thin flake. Gain this and the ledge and climb to the top.

Giant's Ear 20ft. Severe
This is the huge detached flake a few yards right of Dwarf's Ear. The difficulty is gaining the groove between the flake and the main mass of rock.

Eskapade 20ft. Hard V.S. (5b)
This is the groove 5ft. right of Giant's Ear.

Eskalation 20ft. Hard V.S. (5c)
Ascend the overhang and hanging groove 5ft. right of Eskapade.

Green Chimney 25ft. V. Diff.
This chimney runs to an obvious oak tree. Climb to the chockstone then climb the left face to the top.

Green Slab 25ft. Severe
The slab right of the last climb. Climb the right-hand side of the slab to a ledge. Either traverse into Green Chimney or finish up Green Slab's Crack.

Green Slab's Crack 25ft. Severe
The strenuous crack to the right of Green Slab.

Left Unconquerable   25ft.   Severe
The obvious crack a few feet right of Green Slab's Crack. Climb to the ledge and then direct to the top.

Right Unconquerable   25ft.   Hard Severe
Ascend the fine strenuous crack right of the previous climb.

Deception Chimney   25ft.   Diff.
The chimney 10ft. right of the last climb.

Esklets Eliminate   20ft.   Hard V.S. (5b)
Now free, this climb runs up the pegging wall round the arete from the last climb. Start below the obvious nose, gain it, move left then up to the top.

THORGILL CRAG   G.R. 713959

Thorgill Crag lies on the south-west side of Rosedale. The rocks are in an attractive setting and are about 300 yards long.

APPROACHES

The farmer below the crag is opposed to climbers crossing his land and has put up notices to this effect. An alternative approach - less likely to cause problems and suggested to the landowner - would be to take the road from Rosedale Abbey leading to Hutton le Hole up a steep bank. Follow the old railway track along the moor top northwest for about a mile and descend to the top of the crag. However at the time of writing no permission to climb has been given.

It is believed that there may be nesting birds near the crag so the area should be avoided during April to July.

The first climb is on a prominent buttress, split by a crack at the left-hand edge of the crag.

Last Crack   15ft.   Hard V. Diff.
The last buttress on the left of the crag is split by a crack. Climb the wall left of the crack to a ledge, an awkward move into the crack leads to the top.

Variation   Severe
The crack can be gained and climbed from the right.

Vee Corner   12ft.   V. Diff.
Start around the corner 10ft. right of the last crack.

Friends   30ft.   Hard V.S. (5b)
On the buttress right of Vee Corner lies an obvious open groove. Climb the open groove and go direct to the top of the crag.

OTHER CRAGS 155

Square Groove   15ft.   V. Diff.
About 80 yards right of Vee Corner by a square groove above a large boulder. Climb the groove to a tree, step around to the left and gain the top.

Jungle Corner   15ft.   Mod.
The obvious overgrown corner 50ft. right of Square Groove.

Thunder Rock   30ft.   V.S. (5a)
Start 10ft. right of Jungle Corner in the middle of the wall. Ascend the wall by an awkward move and a series of mantleshelves.

Knife   25ft.   Hard V.S. (5b)
Climbs the sharp arete right of Thunder Rock.

Sip   20ft.   Hard Diff.
Start 10ft. right of Thunder Rock. Climb the wall to finish at an oak embedded in the rock.

Corn Flake - left hand   20ft.   Severe
The obvious crackline 50ft. right of Sip. Climb past a holly bush.

Corn Flake - right hand   25ft.   V.S. (4c)
Climb the flake and crack above, 10ft. right of the left-hand crack.

Tough Nut   25ft.   Severe
Starts at the base of chimney 10ft. right of the above route. A hard start leads into the chimney which is followed throughout.

Rosedale Buttress Ordinary   45ft.   Diff.
Rosedale Buttress is the large buttress which in profile resembles a nose. The ordinary route starts about 15ft. left of the lowest rocks. Ascend direct with care.

Rosedale Buttress Direct   45ft.   Hard Diff.
Starts just right of the ordinary route. Climb diagonally right to the nose, follow the crest of the nose to the top. Pleasant.

Banjaxed   40ft.   Hard V.S. (5b)
Start just right of the nose. Scramble up for about 5ft. to an obvious horizontal crack. Hand traverse this for a few feet to a vertical crack. Ascend this to the arete of Rosedale Buttress Direct.

Rambler's Ridge   45ft.   Severe
The isolated rib of rock around the corner right of Rosedale Buttress. Climb the groove in the corner for 20ft. to a stance, belay. Move right to gain the rib which is climbed mainly on its right face to the top.

Roof Crack   Hard V.S. (5a)
A prominent overhang to the right of the last route.

OTHER CRAGS

BRIDESTONES
G.R. 873915

The rocks are situated in a pleasant area of open moorland just north of Dalby Forest. The climbing is in two areas, Lower and Higher Bridestones, with the best routes on the latter.

The rock is a soft sandstone which in places is rather friable.

HISTORY

In 1981/82 Ian Dunn was mainly responsible for the fast development of these rocks after their "discovery" by Stuart Bradley.

ACCESS

The rocks are best reached from Thornton Dale near Pickering. Take the class C road for about one and a half miles to the start of the Dalby Forest drive (£1.00 toll). Follow this through Low Dalby and High Dalby until a car park is reached, on the left, near a small lake on Stainsdale Beck. The car park has Forestry Commission notices giving directions to the rocks.

LOWER BRIDESTONES is the first of the two areas and is useful for bouldering. It consists of several buttresses giving routes up to 15ft. long. Tippling Pinnacle, the obvious leaning tower, has several Hard V.S. routes on it.

HIGHER BRIDESTONES is situated about two thirds of a mile Northwest of the lower Bridestone rocks. They are characterised by a solitary buttress at the point of arrival, and an overhanging escarpment which is naturally divided into four buttresses. The first one described is the most northerly and climbs are listed from left to right.

BUTTRESS 1

Hoedown   15ft.   Hard Severe (4b)
Climb the wall at the extreme north end of the escarpment.

Bat out of Hell   20ft.   Hard V.S. (5a)
The wall 5ft. right of Hoedown.

Dingly Dell   20ft.   Hard V.S. (5b)
Climb the wall diagonally rightwards from the start of the last climb.

Going for the One   25ft.   E2 (5b)
Climb the steep wall past the two poor threads to the roof 6ft. right of Dingly Dell. Climb the roof direct.

Right Side of the Law 20ft. Hard V.S. (5a)
The wall 8ft. right of the last climb.

Bird Shit Groove 20ft. Hard Severe (4b)
Climb the groove at the south end of the buttress.

BUTTRESS 2

Northern Lights 20ft. Severe
Climb the wall at the left edge of the buttress.

Winter Wonderland 25ft. Hard V.S. (5b)
Climb the wall directly behind a boulder in the ground.

Lucky Man 25ft. Hard V.S. (5b)
Starts 30ft. right of the last route. Climb the wall to an obvious undercut at the back of a large roof. Climb the roof, finishing up some friable fluting.

Tainted Love 25ft. Hard V.S. (5b)
Start 8ft. right of Lucky Man and climb the obvious short hanging flake and wall above.

Sambo Pati 20ft. Hard V.S. (5a)
Climb the obvious bubbly weakness right of Tainted Love.

Walk a Thin Line 20ft. V.S. (4c)
Climb the right-hand end of the buttress on bubbly rock.

BUTTRESS 3

Changes 15ft. Hard Severe (4b)
Climb the wall left of the obvious wide crack.

Squeeze and Squirm 20ft. Severe
The obvious off width crack.

Juggler 20ft. Hard V.S. (5a)
The wall immediately right of Squeeze and Squirm.

Audi Quatro 20ft. Hard V.S. (5b)
The wall 6ft. right of Juggler.

Turbo Charged 20ft. Hard V.S. (5b)
Climb the wall with an obvious undercut at the back of the roof 6ft. right of Audi Quatro.

Theft 20ft. Hard V.S. (5b)
Start 10ft. right of the last climb and climb the wall, moving rightwards.

For Someone Very Special   25ft.   Hard V. Diff.
Start at the extreme right of the buttress. Move diagonally left across the slab to the top.

BUTTRESS 4

Just for the record   20ft.   V.S. (4c)
Climb the arete at the left hand edge of the buttress.

Ain't no lullaby   20ft.   Hard V.S. (5b)
Climb the wall 10ft. right of the arete to a triangular overhang.

Wind Up   20ft.   Hard V.S. (5b)
Climb the wall via an obvious slot.

Gordini   20ft.   Hard V.S. (5b)
Climb the wall 8ft. right of the last climb.

Oh Carol   20ft.   Hard V.S. (5b)
Climb the wall and overhang at the righthand end of the buttress.

BUTTRESS 5

The solitary buttress to the south of the escarpment.

Wrong Time of the Month   20ft.   Hard V.S. (5a)
Climb the north face of the buttress on the left.

Vin Rouge   20ft.   Hard V.S. (5a)
Climb the north face on the right.

Honeycomb   20ft.   Severe
Start on a small ledge just off the ground. Climb direct to the top just right of the arete.

Scoop Wall   20ft.   Mild Severe
Start as for Honeycomb and climb the obvious weakness up the west face.

Red Flash   20ft.   V.S. (4c)
Climb the wall 10ft. right of Scoop Wall on pockets.

Strawberry Fields   20ft.   V.S. (4c)
Climb the wall 5ft. right of Red Flash on superb holds.

Scarlet Pimpernel   20ft.   Hard V.S. (5a)
The scoop 5ft. right of Strawberry Fields. Exit on the right.

Red Light 15ft. Hard V.S. (5a)
Climb the arete right of Scarlet Pimpernel. Start on the right.

Little Red Robin Hard V.S. (5b)
A girdle of Red Buttress. Start as for Red Light and traverse to Honeycomb.

NEWTONDALE G.R. 840948

Routes have been recorded on these extensive crags, but due to the unstable nature of the rock they are not recommended.

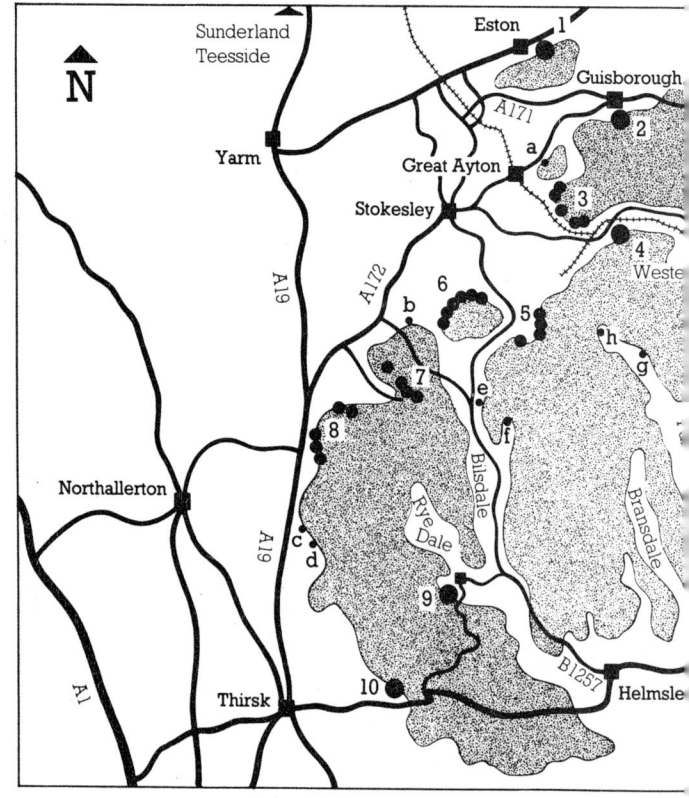